Planning An
African Safari

For The
Everyday Working Man

A Part of the Thorn Bush Series

Planning An
African Safari

For The
Everyday Working Man

Kerry Thomas
Waco, Texas, USA

In collaboration with Paul Stones Safaris
Johannesburg, South Africa

A DVD version of this book is available at www.tomkatproductions.net

Order this book online at www.trafford.com
or email orders@trafford.com

Most Trafford titles are also available at major online book retailers.

© Copyright 2012 Kerry Thomas.
All rights reserved. No part of this publication may be reproduced, stored in a retrieval system, or transmitted, in any form or by any means, electronic, mechanical, photocopying, recording, or otherwise, without the written prior permission of the author.

Printed in the United States of America.

ISBN: 978-1-4669-4059-8 (sc)
ISBN: 978-1-4669-4061-1 (hc)
ISBN: 978-1-4669-4060-4 (e)

Library of Congress Control Number: 2012909819

Trafford rev. 06/14/2012

 www.trafford.com

North America & international
toll-free: 1 888 232 4444 (USA & Canada)
phone: 250 383 6864 ♦ fax: 812 355 4082

Dedication

To my beautiful loving wife Olaiya and my sons Kerry Jr. and Kolton. I want to thank you for your understanding and for tolerating the addiction that I have for Africa. Most of all I thank you for your support. It is because of you that I have found the courage and strength in myself to pursue those things that are just over the horizon.

Pause for the simple things in life.
For these are the things that you will remember the most.
When the conversation turns to safari for the everyday
workingman, there is but one question.
How bad do you want it?
Live life without regret.

Dream. Dare. Explore . . . . Live!

Kerry Thomas
2012

Contents

Foreword xi
Preface xv
Acknowledgments xvii
Deciding to Go to Africa xix

Chapter 1.   Where Do You Want to Hunt? 1
Chapter 2.   What Are the Animals You Want to Take? 5
Chapter 3.   How Long Should You Hunt? 9
Chapter 4.   How Do You Pick Your PH? 13
Chapter 5.   1-1 or 2-1 Hunts 19
Chapter 6.   Outfitter's Questionnaire 21
Chapter 7.   Safari Hunting and Fees 23
Chapter 8.   Time of Year to Go 31
Chapter 9.   Bow versus Rifle 35
Chapter 10. Taxidermy: US versus Africa 39
Chapter 11. Medicines and Vaccinations 45
Chapter 12. Flight Options to South Africa 49
Chapter 13. A Few Things You Should Consider 53
Chapter 14. Guns for Africa 59
Chapter 15. Customs Forms and Rifle Permit 65
Chapter 16. Proper Shot Placement on African Animals 69
Chapter 17. What Do You Need to Pack for Your Safari? 73
Chapter 18. Your Arrival in the Country 77
Chapter 19. What to Expect in Camp 81
Chapter 20. A Typical Hunting Day 85
Chapter 21. After the Animal Is Down 89
Chapter 22. Care of Your Trophies 93
Chapter 23. Activities after the Hunt 95
Chapter 24. It's All about the Money 99

Thoughts on the African Safari 103
Safari Planning Checklist 105
About the Author 107

Foreword

 Africa! The very name itself has at times sent chills down the spine of many a hunter. Africa! She is like a dark and mysterious siren calling out in the minds of most die-hard hunters. Her voice will start to whisper in their ears. Quietly and softly at first notice but all the while demanding to be heard just the same. But alas it appears that she is so far removed from the reaches of the common man that it's barley worth dreaming about. It would seem that one should sooner wish to go to the moon as that might be more possible than actually going on an African safari. How could something so farfetched be possible?

 Writers of the African hunting novels paint a picture that dazzles the imagination and ignites the passion that all hunters share. The word safari means journey. Safari hunting is much, much more than the simple act of taking an animal's life. The very act of killing your prize can even be anticlimactic in some cases. The reasons for going on safari should go far beyond that. The safari experience should encompass the entire quest or process of the hunt itself. Getting a trophy animal is just part of your reward after engaging in a safari. Whether you have a gun in your hand or a camera the goal is always the same. You will have to overcome the challenges of closing the distance between you and your prey. Be it hiking for hours and covering many miles while following the methodical footsteps of your trackers. Or spotting and stalking from the truck. The toughest part is getting inside of the animal's circle of detection to get the shot. Shooting an eland bull two hundred and fifty yards away off of the back of the truck is simply just killing an animal with no real hunting involved. During a proper traditional safari you get the opportunity to get out and enjoy all the natural wonders that Mother Nature has to offer. It's real and it's raw. Now that's what I call hunting. And that my friend is the mystical lure that captivates our imaginations. It's like an invisible force that drives us to seek out the distant destination of Africa.

If you are in it just for the kill and nothing else don't waste your time on Africa. You can save the money on airfare and daily rates by just hunting an exotic game ranch in the states. But remember telling the tales of your adventures will be less colorful on a state side game ranch hunt. I often find myself reminiscing about some of my past adventures. While on safari I was once run out of my ground blind by an overly curious black mamba. Also on the occasion when it felt like time stood still in the bush. It was the first time that I tipped toed within forty-five yards of a pair of larger than life rhinos just to take a photo. Or the heart-pounding moments when I watched a pair of cheetahs creep and crawl closer and closer to a small herd of zebra at a waterhole. There was water splashing with hooves and dust everywhere as the hunter and prey matched wits. Then there was the time I got a little too close to the biggest bull elephant that I have ever seen. That encounter resulted in me and my party running for our very lives from a somewhat frustrated elephant. I can tell you that experiencing these events and many others like them are priceless. They will stay with me and be told and retold in vivid detail until the day I die. To me that is what safari is all about. I would not trade those times for sitting in a box blind on a canned hunt anywhere.

All of this brings me back to one word. Africa! Her red sand will indeed get in your blood. The natural beauty of the land and her people are incredibly intoxicating. For decades safari has often been thought of as a sport for the super rich. I am here to tell you that is not the case. Can an African safari be expensive? I won't try to fool you here. The answer is yes it can be. But like most things in this world it will vary in price. Costs will be dependent on a lot of variables. The biggest of which will be in what you want to hunt. But what I will say is it can be done at a reasonable expense. The very wealthy hunters in their three piece suits in the high rise office building may decide to take a twenty-one day safari on a whim. After he's made up his mind he will simply write a check for his expenses and be on his way. The rest of us will have to do as they say in Africa *"make a plan"* to put our hunts together piece by painstaking piece.

Paying attention to the details and staying focused are the first orders of business. With some hard work you will soon realize that you yourself can live out the dream for an African safari. Do understand it will be a lot of work. If you can believe it you can achieve it. After all there's a reason it's called a hunt of a lifetime.

There is a method to the madness of safari planning. By the time you finish this book you will have a very good grasp on the process. With a proper plan in place in time you too can enjoy a safari. This book will give you an understanding of what is necessary for your entire trip from conception to completion. There are a great many stones that must be turned over before you can call it done. You should also recognize and accept one thing. That is once you are in Africa you will spend your last few days pondering in the back of your mind how can I come back. I can tell you that a safari and an elephant are a lot alike. They are both big in size and can be overwhelming. I was once asked "how do you eat an elephant?" The answer is one bite at a time! And that is how you should go about the planning of your safari. One bite at a time. You have in your hands dozens of pages covering many years of hard lessons learned as well as first hand experiences of well laid plans. Your commitment to the planning for your African safari starts now. It can be a reality before you know it. You just have to take that first bite.

And always remember what the monkey said when he got his tail cut off? *"It won't be long now"*

Kerry Thomas
Waco, Texas
May, 2012

PREFACE

The author, Kerry Thomas.

I am not a celebrity hunter that gets paid to hunt. I am not a rich or wealthy man by any means. I am a man with dirt under his fingernails. I am a man that, like most, works hard every day and who had to save for years to make his first safari happen. The information found here was gathered through my experiences in planning my safaris over the past few years. It is a very detailed business of planning and executing a hunt in South Africa. I wanted to "unmuddy the waters" for those who've shared the same dream for a safari as I have for so many years but didn't know where to start. With the information I am providing, I will help you to avoid the many pitfalls that plague so many hunters as well as the overlooked details that can turn a trip of a lifetime into a nightmare. Please understand that it is not my intent to present this information as the only way to go about planning your safari. These are simply the lessons that I learned along the way. With the help of my good friend Paul Stones of Paul Stones Safaris in South Africa, I would like to share them with you.

Acknowledgments

It is with great appreciation that I would like to thank Paul Stones of Paul Stones Safaris in South Africa. His knowledge of South Africa and the time we spent hunting together helped me immensely in my research.
Thank you to my lifelong friend Paul Nardell for working so hard to get the shots and for going "all the way to Johannesburg."
And I would also like to thank and give credit to my friend Russell Maclaughlin for contributing the cover photography.

Deciding to Go to Africa

An impala ram browsing on scrub brush during the dry season.

The task of planning your safari is monumental. So before doing so, you should first ask yourself why do you want to hunt Africa? Is it the adventure of being in a place known for her wild remote country? A place that calls to the big game hunter trapped inside all of us. Africa means a variety of things to a lot of different people. For some, it's almost like a pilgrimage back to the cradle of hunting. Are you looking for record book trophies? Or something different from what your buddies have hanging on their walls? Do you want to hunt plains game or maybe step up to dangerous game? Are you out for a bigger adventure than what you can find sitting in a deer blind waiting for a whitetail?

You could spend a week in Alaska hunting one grizzly bear or you could spend eight days hunting one elk in the mountains of Colorado. Or do you, like myself, want to hunt for eight to ten days and have the opportunity to take a different animal every day. You will see dozens of animals during the course of your hunt, many different species.

On the trail headed to the top of a ridge are professional hunter Paul Stones and his two trackers followed by the author.

If you are looking for adventure such as that written in the books from big name game hunters of yesteryear, you may be setting yourself up for a big disappointment. The stories in the books describe walking with a dozen porters carrying equipment and hunting for weeks or even months at a time, living off the land as you go. For the most part, those days are long gone. While you can still find an "as wild as it gets type" safari, most first-time hunters are not able to afford to go into the remote reaches of some of the more rugged countries to do so. Before you ever set foot in Africa, you probably already have a preconceived image in your mind of what safari means to you. It is difficult for the first-time hunter to have a gauge of what is to be expected on a hunt. The cost of travel for charter flights from the airport to some of the more remote camps alone can be more than the airfare from the US that gets you to South Africa. But don't despair; you can still have a wonderful time on a modern-day hunt.

You now have taken in your hands the first step in making sure you get the experience that you dreamed of.

CHAPTER 1

Where Do You Want to Hunt?

A map of the main hunting countries in southern Africa.

Now that we understand the "why we hunt," let's discuss the "where in Africa do you want to hunt." There are many different countries in Africa to choose from—South Africa, Namibia, Zimbabwe, Botswana, Mozambique, Tanzania, Zambia, etc. Each country has a variety of big game species to choose from, many of which will overlap while others will be exclusive to a particular area. If there is a particular animal that you are after, you should take the time find out where that animal is most commonly found. Let's take the bongo for example. It's generally only found deep in the forest areas of Central Africa. So if there is an outfitter offering you a free-range bongo hunt in southern Namibia, that should raise a red flag with you. He may only have a couple that he bought for you and one other client to shoot. Beware of this guy. He is probably trying to pull a fast one on you.

But our focus here is mainly in the pursuit of plains game found in South Africa. The availability of most any game animal can be found in South Africa.

Next we'll talk about the size of the concessions. The size of the concessions in South Africa will vary widely. Concessions are similar to what we call a hunting lease here in the States. Generally, the areas will range from five thousand to well over twenty-five thousand acres. With that being said, you will want to hunt an area that is at least ten thousand acres. Personally, I would look for a twenty thousand–acre property as a minimum. There are outfitters that will advertise that they have twenty thousand, forty thousand, or even one hundred thousand–plus acres to hunt on. Ask questions. Find out if it is all one area or will you be spreading your hunting over several small properties. They tend to mislead their hunt services as being conducted on one large hunting area when actually it is on four or five smaller ones. Make sure you ask questions. There will be occasions that you will be hunting in several areas depending on the game you're after. This is a normal practice: you just know up front before you go what you are getting.

Bear in mind that pretty much all concessions in South Africa are going to be high fenced. On a good concession, the only fence you should come in contact with is the main gate when you enter. Although most people don't want to hunt in a fence, a twenty-five thousand–acre game ranch covers over thirty-eight square miles. Many of the game species may only range about four to five square miles; therefore, many of them may never know that the fences exists. You can easily hunt for a week and never see the fence.

You don't want to be involved in what is known as a "goats in gates hunt." You are not hunting on a real game ranch. You are hunting on farm that has wildlife on it. You will be driving through cattle and sheep camps. That is not fun, and that is not why you go to Africa.

Most of the hunting in South Africa occurs in the northern areas of the Limpopo Province and the eastern part of the country. These areas are rich in game, and the hunting industry is strong. Most of the southern part of South Africa will not give you the landscape that you would expect of Africa.

CHAPTER 2

What Are the Animals You Want to Take?

A Burchell's zebra mare heavy with foal.

The different styles of hunting can vary worldwide. But hunting is still hunting when properly done in a manner that gives the prey a fighting chance. There are basically two types of safari hunts in Africa. Your choices are either plains game or dangerous game.

Dangerous game consists of the elephant, lion, leopard, rhino, and buffalo, better known as the big five. Also added to the list should be the hippo and crocodile. Countries such as Botswana, Tanzania, Mozambique, Zambia, and Zimbabwe are a better choice for hunting the big five species due to the availability of enormous government-owned hunting areas. Animals here will mostly be free ranging and very much wild. The hunting of any of theses animals will be very expensive in comparison to the hunting of plains game. Most first-time game safari goers will be after a plains game hunt. To give you an idea, a leopard hunt will be in the $12,000 range and up. A lion will be in the $20,000 range and up. For that type of money, you could hunt a truckload of plains game.

Some of Africa's most sought-after plains game consists of the following: kudu, with its beautiful long spiraling horns; the eland, the largest of the African antelope; nyala, with it's unique markings; waterbuck, with long sweeping horns; blue and black wildebeest, also know as the clowns of the plains due to their constant frolicking display. Gemsboks are one of the staple symbols of Africa with its very long and very sharp three-foot long horns and no hunts complete without an impala.

After getting an uneasy feeling an old impala ram tests the wind for danger.

Others included will be the sable, roan, bushbuck, red hartebeest, blesbuck, reedbuck, duikers, grysbok, klipspringer steenbok, Hartmann's and Burchell's zebra, bushpig, giraffe, vervet monkey, baboon, warthog. Africa has several small cat species that can be hunted such as the African wildcat, civet, serval, and caracal.

Most decent properties will have a minimum of about fifteen or more different species available to hunt. Again, not all species will be on one property, so some travel between properties may be required to hunt the particular ones that you're after.

The quality of trophy in which you desire should be addressed next. For some, such as myself, any respectable representation of the hunted species is a trophy. Now that's not to say I don't want a monster kudu trophy hanging on my wall. I believe that if you go to Africa with the focus of only shooting an animal that is a record book trophy you will not have a good trip. If you have chosen a PH or "professional hunter" well, he will not let you shoot an inferior animal. A PH's worst nightmare is a hunter showing up with a gun in one hand and a record book in the other, expecting or rather demanding to shoot the biggest horns in Africa. This type of hunter may see a lot of animals, but if the PH has any doubt at all that it may not meet the client's demands, he will pass on it. Since the hunter has made it clear that he wants a specific size trophy, the PH probably won't want to take a chance. For example, I've seen a hunter show up and demand a twenty-eight-inch impala and nothing less. During the course of the hunt, the hunter may pass up several good twenty-six to twenty-seven inchers, only to have to settle for a twenty-five inches on the last day rather than go home empty-handed. Remember that if the PH is having a good time hunting with you and you are having a good time hunting with him, it will seem like you are hunting with an old friend. He may be inclined to go the extra mile for you on doing the little things that otherwise may have been overlooked. If you come across as an arrogant and demanding person, your PH may see you as more of a chore to be around rather than a pleasure to hunt with. At that point, you are just another client that must be dealt with. Don't be the person that shows up bragging about how good of a shot you are. The PH doesn't want to hear it. He has had hundreds of hunters before you that have all sang the same song. So have honest expectations and be honest with the PH. You will have a good trip if you do that.

What are the numbers of trophies animals on quota? Game ranches in South Africa take animals off according to a quota system. Once a year, they will use helicopters to fly over or use other means to count the animals that they have on the property. They may count 150 kudu bulls but determine that there are, say, fifty-five bulls that are mature enough to shoot. Of the fifty-five bulls, they may only allow five to be taken off the property this hunting season. Once those five are taken off, no others will be allowed until after the game count next year and a new quota has been established. By doing this, the quality of trophy animal is kept high. This is done for all species on the game ranch. Not only do you continue to get high quality mature animals, you also maintain good management numbers that keep overpopulation down.

Always alert, the kudu bull has his radarlike ears poised at attention; also known as the gray ghost.

CHAPTER 3

How Long Should You Hunt?

Safari calendar with hunting and travel dates.

The average hunt will usually be eight, ten, or fourteen days. The length of the hunt will be determined on the number of animals that you want to take. As a general rule of thumb, you should allow at least one day per animal that you want to hunt. There may be a day or two that you will be able to get more than one animal in a day but don't count on it. You will see a lot of animals. Some of them will be too small while others may have a broken horn tip from fighting. Your PH and trackers will do their jobs by taking the time to look them over, making sure they're worthy of a stalk and a shot. Keep in mind that you may have to make several attempted stalks before you close the deal. You may be slipping in on a zebra stallion when a bedded down impala that you never saw blows at you, sending the zebra over the next ridge. Some outfitters will require a minimum number of days of hunting depending on what you are hunting. Most all dangerous game hunts will require a minimum of twelve days, generally speaking. Some dangerous game such as elephant may be as much as twenty-one days. A plains game hunt will sometimes have a ten-day hunt requirement on it, depending on the species you are after. For example, an outfitter might not let you hunt a sable on a ten-day hunt. They would normally want fourteen days to hunt a sable bull. One reason for this is to allow time for looking over all the different animals you will encounter. Another reason is the part of the value that the outfitter has attached to the animal. Something else to consider is that on a ten-day hunt, you will be gone from home for approximately fourteen days. There is a day and a half of travel at the beginning of you trip and a half of a day in camp depending on the distance from airport to camp. The same applies when you leave South Africa. Be sure you understand this. So unless you plan with your PH specifically for travel days in the beginning and end your ten-day hunt will only be about nine days. By this, I mean the day of arrival and the day of departure are considered half days on your hunt even though you may not hunt at all. This is a small but commonly overlooked detail. My suggestion is to plan for as long of a hunt as you can afford. My theory behind this is that this safari will be the hunt of a lifetime, and you may only be able to do it one time. So you should plan as though you may never go back. I'll touch on more on why you should think this way later.

Kerry Thomas posing next to one of many termite mounds found near the safari camp.

If you bag all your animals before your hunt is over, make prior plans with your PH for a plan B for a sightseeing, maybe get some fishing in on your trip or check out one of the national parks. Or simply spend your last days taking in the camp property taking photos or relaxing. These are moments you will reflect on for years to come after the hunt is over. So take my advice and soak them up.

CHAPTER 4

How Do You Pick Your PH?

PH Paul Stones and Kerry Thomas relaxing during a midmorning snack break.

A PH is a "professional hunter." He is the person that takes you out on your hunt every day and is the one who takes care of your day-to-day needs while in his care on the safari. He is not there to do your hunt for you. He is there to assist you in finding what you are looking for and to make sure the laws are abided by. He will be your companion for the duration of your stay in the safari and will get you in position on a good animal. Making the shot is still on your shoulders. If there is a problem that needs to be addressed, talk to him. If for example you don't smoke and one of the trackers lights up a cigarette on the back of the truck, talk to him. Don't wait until a little problem festers into a bigger issue before saying something.

The outfitter is the person that owns the safari company and often the property on which the hunt is conducted. He will either conduct the hunts himself or hire another PH to run them for him. In some cases, the PH may also be the outfitter. Obviously, word of mouth is the very best way to find a PH. If you know of anyone that has ever gone on a safari, that is the first place to start. I've never met a hunter that did not want to talk about his exploits on the Dark Continent. Here are a few questions you can ask. He can let you know if his PH was worth hunting with or not. Ask him what he hunted. What was the quality of the trophies that he took? How much game did he see? What were the camp conditions like? How well was he treated by the staff? How was the food in camp? Did he do everything that he promised he would do? Remember, it is up to you to ask the questions. By asking lots of questions, you will quickly be able to see if the person that you are talking to is on their game or is just blowing smoke in your face.

Meeting PH Paul Stones at the SCI convention in Las Vegas to work out the details of the upcoming hunt.

Another way to go would be the hunter's shows. The hunter's shows are great places to meet outfitters from all over the world. The Dallas Safari Club and Safari Club International are probably two of the best conventions to attend. There, you can talk face to face with the person that you will actually be hunting with and see videos and photos of prior hunts as well as pick up brochures so that you can later compare them to one another. You should never go to the show looking to book a hunt right then and there with an outfitter or PH that you just met. Remember, you should be on a fact-finding mission. Some outfitters will offer you a special show deal for a safari that is only good if you book it right this moment and is withdrawn if you walk away. You should walk away from this outfitter. No respectable outfitter would use this used car salesman's angle to try to get you to book a hunt. There are just too many variables that have to be worked out before you should commit to a hunt. Take you time and ask lots of questions. In the end, you will get what you pay for.

Now we look at taking the Internet route. This is where the research begins to get thick. The Internet search engines can yield a massive amount of results. Where do you start? One problem with using the Internet only is that you don't get to meet the outfitter face to face. You are just going by what's on the site. You can and should research the area that they are in and see if they fit the bill for what you are after. See if there are references available. You should not get blinded by a dazzling website during your search. Check prices, location, travel time to camp, available game, and so on. International phone calls can be expensive, and then there's a time zone difference from about six to ten hours. So you should e-mail any questions you have. Also, you need to start a spreadsheet. Place the outfitter's list that you are looking at across the top. Place the species you want going down the side. This way, you can compare apples to apples on the price of each animal and have a running total at the bottom. If you are not very computer savvy, this can also be done on a pad of paper. Keep in mind that different areas may warrant a difference in price. This is due to the availability of the animals in the region and quality of animals to be found there. Try to weigh these into your decision. Don't forget it's the details that will make or break your trip. The more research that's done, the less there is left to chance.

What are the characteristics of a good PH? You should expect your PH to be able to answer all your basic questions and request without any problems. He should offer up references readily and not hesitate in doing so. He should be a member of the Professional Hunters' Association of South Africa or the International Professional Hunters Association. Does he ask you what you are looking for in a safari in reference to trophy quality, accommodations, or expectations of the safari experience itself? He should let you know up front that, for example, "Yes, we do have caracal cats but the odds of getting one will be slim. Or we may have to do some traveling to another property to get your gemsbok."

Is he the kind of person you would be able to virtually live with for ten or twelve days? If you get a funny vibes during a visit, a hunting show could spell disaster in the bush. Follow your gut instinct on this. His primary focus should be on making sure that you are taken care of and not just trying to get your money.

For most, the hard part is not knowing the right questions to ask a PH. Many outfitters will tell a client what they want to hear. This is where doing your homework will pay off. Here are some questions you may want to ask a potential PH.

1. Ask for a price list of all the available animals he has on quota. Are the animals naturally occurring in that area? If not, does this pose an issue with you? Remember, you are going to Africa to get a real African experience. You could hunt zebra here in the US if it's just about the animals.

2. Ask how many clients he hunts within a year. Try to get a feel if he is focused on fewer quality hunts or overfilling his camp week after week to maximize his dollar. I personally would not want to hunt with a PH that treats his camp as a fast-food franchise by running as many hunters through as he can. A PH with fewer clients may be able to give you more of his attention and make your trip much more memorable, but in a positive way. Understand that he is in business to make money, but there should be some integrity in what he does.

3. Ask him to show you on a map where the property or properties are located. A lot of South Africa looks like the US as far as the plains and rolling hills. You need to ask if it's the real Africa. Will I have a chance to see elephant or buffalo, and are there lions in the area?

4. How long has he been a PH?
5. How many people does he have working for him?
6. What is camp like?
7. What is the food like in camp?
8. Will there be other hunters in camp with you?
9. Will there be phone or Internet service in camp?
10. Who will pick you up from the airport?
11. Always ask for and check his references.
12. Find out if he will be the one with you in camp or will you be hunting with another PH that works for him. You should never be sent out with just a tracker to hunt.
13. Let the outfitter know that you are serious about hunting in Africa, what your target date is, and about how much your budget is going to be. There are a lot of "tire kickers" at these shows pretending that they are big time hunters and high rollers. These guys walk around grabbing literature from every booth they pass by not bothering to see where the companies are from or what they have to offer. Don't be afraid to stop and talk to them. That's why they are there. But on the other hand, don't' waste yours or their time acting like a big shot talking about a $30,000 lion hunt that you know you can't afford. This is why you've narrowed down your country of choice. Remember, you're on a mission to get info on a specific area or country. Again, it's your safari, so ask a lot questions.

Chapter 5

1-1 or 2-1 Hunts

Putting together a game plan from high above the valley floor.

1-1 with your PH or 2-1? You should plan to hunt 1-1 with your own PH. What this means is that it will be just you and your PH and no other hunter. A 2-1 may be you, your buddy, and the PH. 2-1 hunts are tough on the PH and sometimes not very productive for either of the hunters. 1-1 will give you the best chance of getting all the animals that you came to get.

Most outfitters will have a discounted price if you do a 2-1 hunt. Remember, when you book a safari, it's all about you and what you want from your trip. It's not about anybody else. Don't go the cheap route. The outfitter may say, "Hey, if you bring your buddy, I'll knock off fifty bucks a day." On a ten-day hunt, it's $1,000 between the two of you. But when your buddy wounds his eland bull on day 2 and you haven't shot anything yet. You may spend the next three days tracking that bull, which can happen. You will hate that buddy for the rest of your life. For every day that goes by that you don't hunt, there's another fifty dollars that you could have spent and had your own PH. You must have a long hard talk with your buddy before going 2-1. Especially if he's not a very good shot just know that it could take ten minutes or days to find it. Before you know it, there goes half of your safari.

You are better off to save a bit longer in order to do a proper 1-1 safari. You will avoid the tension and the risk of losing your buddy as a friend.

You might also think about going on a cull hunt. A cull hunt is one in which you have the opportunity to shoot nontrophy animals usually at a discounted price. They may have broken horns or they may be females. This is just another means for the ranch owner to get his numbers in check. The daily rate, which we will cover a little later, may be reduced; but this is not always the case.

A mother warthog and her offspring quench their thirst with a drink of water in the midday heat.

CHAPTER 6

Outfitter's Questionnaire

The bleached skull of a cape buffalo hanging on the fence
near the camp's fire pit.

At some point, your PH will ask you to fill out an outfitter's questionnaire. This form will answer vital questions that he needs to know about you while you are in his care.

Dietary restrictions should be addressed. Any allergies to food that you have need to be mentioned on this form. If there are religious restrictions on meats, let him know. The PH will make sure the camp staff doesn't include them in your meals. It's basically a list of likes and don't likes.

Any special requests will also be listed. Your PH will want to know if you have a list of you special request such as wines, liquors, soft drinks, or other items. If you prefer to have something special in your room, ask for it. Most reasonable request can usually be accommodated.

Information on your medical conditions will be asked. If you have a medical condition or medication that is required to take, you should list it as well. Should something happen to you, your PH will need to know what actions to take on your behalf. Included in this section will be a list of emergency contact numbers and other information about you.

You will be asked to sign a liability release form. The liability release or indemnity form is just what the name implies. It states that you realize and accept that coming to Africa and going into the wild backcountry is dangerous. If you get bitten, trampled, trip over a rock, or otherwise injured, etc., you will not hold the PH or outfitter responsible. By signing this form, you are assuming the risk should the unfortunate happen. This is not to say that the PH is not going to do everything in his power to keep you safe, but sometimes things happen that are out of his control. I will address some measures you should consider later on.

Chapter 7
Safari Hunting and Fees

An elk hunting camp nestled in the Rocky Mountains
of the southwestern corner of Colorado.

The affordability of a safari is often the subject of many hunting camps. There are a lot of people out there that say you can hunt Africa for the price for trophy whitetail or elk. When people think of African safari, they think, "I could never afford that" or "Maybe someday when I hit the lottery." If you are an avid whitetail hunter, you could make it a reality in just a few years with some strategic planning. My method is this, instead of spending $1,500–$2,000 a year on a deer lease. Skip a few years and take the money you would have spent and put it away. You can still hunt your deer, but do it on public land. Most everyone has public land within a reasonable driving distance that you can hunt for free. For years, I've hunted for whitetail on a couple ten thousand–acre areas belonging to the Army Corps of Engineers. It's free to the public; you mostly come and go as you please. Not all public lands will have the monsters that may be found on some of your high-end deer leases, but we have to look at the bigger picture here. The money for the lease, the protein supplement, the corn, the fuel spent driving back and forth checking on things, and the cost of the blinds that you hunt in. Then there's taxidermy for yet another mount that is similar to the ones you and your buddies already have on the wall. Believe me, all the little things add up in just a few years—they will definitely add up. A weeklong elk hunt could easily cost you $4,000 and up, and you only get one elk! The same goes for a trophy whitetail or mule deer. I could go on and on. I'm not saying that you will be able to completely pay for a safari, but this method will get you very close. And the once-in-a-lifetime experience that you'll take away from safari is unmatched by any other.

What is the daily rate? The daily rate is the money that you pay to your PH for his services. There are plains game rates and dangerous game rates. Dangerous game rates will always be higher than plains game due to the added elements of danger and additional work and planning involved in obtaining you trophy. There are also observer rates. This is for anyone on the hunt with you that is not hunting, such as a spouse or friend. This is a reduced rate below the standard daily rate. Daily rate services will usually include the following:

    a. All accommodations and meals while in his care on the safari.
    b. Beverages including alcohol consumed in moderation, and that's after the hunt is finished for the day. There will be no drinking during the hunting day. If you're looking for a place

to party like in some deer camps, safari is not the place for it. There are a lot of accidents that could happen to you or others while in an intoxicated state and your PH does not want to be responsible for babysitting you.

c. Daily laundry services. Your clothes will be laundered on a daily basis in most camps. This means that there is no need to pack excessive clothing. We will cover more on this later.

d. Any required basic game hunting license for your hunt. Some special permitted animals may require additional fees on your part. Again, this is why we do our homework in picking areas, species, and asking lots of questions before the hunt.

e. You will also get the services of a qualified, licensed PH as well as his field staff including game trackers, skinners, and a hunting vehicle. Along with them is also the encampment staff.

f. Proper field preparation of the trophies and skins will be a part of the daily rate.

g. And lastly, transportation of your hunting trophies to a local African taxidermist. All animals must be dipped before being crated and shipped to the US. We will cover more on the taxidermy later.

A rustic safari bush camp located in the northern Limpopo Province.

Some outfitters will sell their safaris based on the luxury of their camp. When an outfitter sits down with you and spends more time talking about the camp instead of the hunting experience, you have to be aware and start asking questions. Even the nicest camp can turn into a nightmare if you are in a camp with people you don't want to be in camp with. If the area and the camp are big enough you could possibly have another hunter or party in camp without any friction. Just make sure you are aware of this up front. The outfitter will have an idea of the personalities of the people he has put together in both parties. He may not know for sure that you will get along, but he has an idea. If possible, I would still try to get the camp to myself even if it meant switching my safari dates by a week of so.

If the outfitter contacts you two months before the safari date and says, "I have a hunter that had to cancel and wants to make up his date. Do you mind if he hunts in your camp with another PH?" Talk to your outfitter about your feelings on the subject on how it will affect your hunt. If you say no there's not much he can do about it. Remember, as much as it's your experience, try to understand that the PH is just trying to make a living and that hunting is his livelihood.

What are trophy fees? The price that you pay to shoot the animal is your trophy fee. Each animal has its own price, and some will vary according to its trophy status or level. As I stated before, the area and the number and size of trophy animals available will have a bearing on the fee that's charged. If the trophy fee is high for a particular animal, it may be because the animals are usually prolific and they are very good. If you find a very low trophy fee, you should be aware of some things.

What is the number of animals in the area? You don't want to arrive in an area to get your primary specie and find out, "Yes, we have them but not very many." You need to know what the chances are of getting your animal. It's one thing if the wind was wrong or you couldn't get in position for the shot. Hunting is hunting, but you still need a fair crack at the animal. For example, some outfitters charge, let's say, $1,800 for a kudu bull that is less than fifty-four inches. A bull measuring over that length may have a trophy fee of $2,200 on him. This is information that you will want to weigh in on your spreadsheet to help you make an educated decision on where you will hunt and who with. Personally, I prefer a pricing system with one set price per animal regardless of it size.

What about package hunts? Package hunts are usually very appealing at first glance. They will have the daily rate rolled in with the trophy fees for the animals in the package. It will appear to be a sweet deal. But you should take a hard look at the animals being offered. A lot of the time, there will be four to five animals in the deal. They will probably include the smaller species like steenbok or duiker with maybe an impala or warthog thrown in. These are the get-you-there animals. Sometimes there might even be a blue or black wildebeest as the main attraction. When you get to Africa for the first time, you will likely have never seen the animals in the package in real life. The animals that he puts you on during your hunt will most likely not be the best of the bunch. That's why the outfitter can offer you such a great deal on the package. You're not going through all the trouble of your safari just to get a couple of small animals. Most outfitters are expecting you to buy some of the more expensive, more desirable species once you get there. Taking something extra is not a problem, but substituting animals in the package is usually not allowed. Understand that for most outfitters, you will pay the entire package price whether you get the opportunity to shoot them all or not. This is why I would not recommend a package hunt. But if you find a package you like, be sure you understand the payment agreement.

The other option is à la carte. À la carte is usually the better way to go. You will pay a daily rate for each day of your hunt and you don't have to pay for the animals until you shoot. You get a copy of the price list from the PH then you can pick and choose what you want to take, though you should have done your choosing long before you left the states. It is still a good idea to take the price list with you for a reference in the field. Providing the quota is there, you may decide not to shoot the gemsbok you thought you wanted so badly. Instead you take a waterbuck that you never entertained the thought of shooting up until the moment you saw one standing there. Believe me it happens.

The number of people in your group will sometimes make a difference on pricing. There is usually a group discount to be had if there are enough people in you hunting party. The outfitter wants a full camp. He may offer as discount for as few as four hunters. As I mentioned before, be sure to find out if your group will be the only ones in camp. I know as the saying goes, "the more the merrier," but this is not always the case. A group of hunters from Russia may have different personal views as your group from southern Alabama. Sharing a camp could get uncomfortable, and there goes your hunt of a lifetime.

There are also transfer fees. Your PH may charge you a transfer fee to pick you up at the airport and take you to camp. If the hunting camp is only a couple of hours away, he may not charge you a fee at all. But if he has to drive you for five or six hours one way, you could expect it. This is where the half day of hunting comes in that I made mention of earlier. You may be charged the half day in instead of a transfer fee depending on the situation.

Tipping

PH Paul Stones on tipping: You will be with your PH and the trackers for the entire safari. You might have a driver with you. You might have a game scout with you in certain parts of the country. At the end of your safari, there's always the question of gratuity. A gratuity is exactly that. It is a thank-you for services over and above the norm. Everybody that you work with on a safari is paid to do his or her job—from the professional hunter down to the lady that cleans your room. It is not your responsibility to fund salaries. Whatever you choose to leave at the end of your safari is your personal choice. If you want to leave the camp staff something extra, it's your choice. If you decided not to leave anything at all, that is still your choice. Nothing will happen to you. Your trophies will get to the taxidermist, and they will get home. You will get back to the airport. Your PH is paid for that service. Anything that is out of the ordinary suggestive wise or little hints dropped, you should get with your outfitter immediately. Tell your PH that you need to speak to the outfitter and he will arrange it for you. There are people out there that like to drop hints during your safari. That is something that should not be tolerated by you or the outfitter.

So if you want to leave a tip, what's a ballpark on the amount of money? For a camp that has a ten-person staff, $700 is a starting point. From there, you could go up, go down, go nothing. It's your call. As far as your PH is concerned, $500 is a good place to start. Again up, down, or nothing at your discretions and no one should tell you differently. If you are booked and are hunting with the outfitter, he should not require a tip. He makes his money on the safari, that is what he does for a living.

If for example you wound an animal and your tracker does an exceptional job in finding him after tracking him for a mile, you may want to slip him something extra—be it ten or twenty dollars, don't do it. Although the tracker found it, there are a lot more people involved in the hunting exercise than just him. It creates a lot of displeasure among other staff members. Rather, wait until the end of the safari and have your PH fill out slips of paper with each of the camp staff member's name on it. You will then be able to give your tip directly to them and know that they are going to get it. Just because you leave a tip with the PH does not mean that the staff will receive it.

Chapter 8

Time of Year to Go

A small herd of blue or brindled wildebeest looking for relief from the unrelenting African sun.

Choosing the time of year to go may come with other outside variables. Some of which will include things such as the availability of your vacation, family commitments, and so on. Although the South African hunting season is basically year round, most of the hunting is done between the months of March and November. Most people don't realize that the seasons in South Africa are opposite of ours. March, April, and May are their fall months. July, August, and September are considered their winter months. December through February is going to be the hottest part of the year for them. Although you could feasibly hunt, there are few people that try to endure the African summer heat hunting. If you dare to attempt a hunt during the hottest part of the year, you risk the chance of hair slipping and other damage to your trophy skins, rendering them unmountable.

Let's compare early-season versus late-season hunting. The early season will give you first crack at the selection of animals. But this is usually not that big of an issue in most cases. If the property is large enough and the numbers are there, you will still have ample opportunity to get a good trophy, be it early or late. For the first few months of the year, you will find that a lot of the PHs and outfitters will be busy traveling. Most will be in the US doing hunter's shows and visiting clients. So if you don't get the opportunity to make one of the hunter's shows, there is a chance that your chosen PH may be in your neck of the woods at some point. You should only try to set an appointment with a PH when you are ready to book with him. It would be unreasonable for you to ask for visits from PHs at random while trying to decide whom to choose. It is very expensive for them to fly all over the US. This would be OK once you have narrowed your list down to just a couple of choices, but you don't want to be the "tire kicker" that I mentioned earlier.

Some other plus and minuses to hunting early season is the thick green vegetation. The rains will have made everything grow heavily, giving you more cover to stalk through. But on the other hand, it makes the animals that much tougher to spot and gives them more places to hide. Given this, you will not be able to pass up as many animals as you could later in the season. Early April and May are usually fairly easier times to book your hunt. That is because the more seasoned safari hunters will usually pick a date later in the late season.

Opportunities with late season hunting can provide plenty of action as well as the early season. One of the best things about late-season hunting is that the animals are definitely easier to spot from a distance. The bad thing is getting close will be a challenge but not impossible. I have hunted the early as well as the late, and I much more prefer the late.

If you are planning to take a teenage son or daughter, the mid-season may be what you are after due to the summer break in school. July and August are going to be the peak season for hunting pretty much across the board. Outfitters will book up faster for this time period; therefore, it is in your best interest to book as soon as you can to lock in your date.

Let's take a brief look at the weather. Early season weather will vary depending on the area and elevation. The mornings will sometimes be a little chilly with temperatures in the fifties. Then they will soon rise up into the seventies very quickly. So you may have to have on a light jacket on the back of the truck when you first leave in the morning. But then, by, say, eight thirty to nine o'clock, you will be shedding clothes. Seventy degrees in South Africa can feel pretty warm, but later on that evening as the sun starts to dip, it will cool down just as quickly as it warmed up.

Late-season weather will be a bit colder on the mornings. The afternoons will be pleasant in the sixty-degrees range on most days. Unlike our North American whitetail that get out and get on the move when it's cold, the African species tend to bed down more.

Almost everyone has this question. What about the creatures that move about without legs? So let's take a moment to look at snakes—"Mr. No-Shoulders."

I have personally had encounters with Rinkhals spitting cobra, puff adders, boomslang, and black mamba snakes on my first safari. It's a wonder I would want to go back. On my second safari, I never saw so much as a snake track. Mind you, I was in two different areas but I attribute it to an early-season versus a late-season hunt. It stands to reason that if you are in the early season with warmer weather, you may have a slightly greater chance of seeing a snake. There will always be a chance of encountering a snake or two no matter what time of year you go. But the same would apply to parts of the US in regards to rattlesnakes. Listen to your PH and keep an eye out for them just as you would at home and you should be all right.

The bush is a natural breeding ground for insects (flies and mosquitoes). Some considerations should be made for these insects. Flies and mosquitoes can sometimes be a real problem when the temperatures start to rise. You should remember to take some type of repellent that contains deet. Personally I'm not that much into all the scent control products, but I would try to go unscented if possible. Remember, you hunt with your nose in the wind, so scent control should not be that big of an issue. There are small biting flies that can be relentless once they get started, so be prepared. Also mosquitoes are how malaria is spread if you are in a malaria area. Although most of South Africa is malaria free.

Chapter 9

Bow versus Rifle

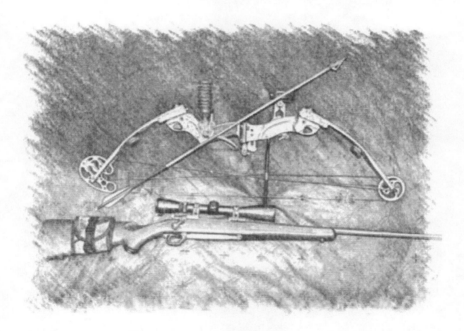

The author's compound bow and his favorite
.270 caliber all-around/safari rifle.

Deciding to hunt with a bow or a rifle. This can be a tough decision for some people. One should take in consideration the extra luggage fee if you decide to take both as well as the odds of success. It's no secret there will be a sizable expense and extensive planning to make your trip happen. In my opinion, you should give yourself your best odds for getting your money's worth.

First, let's look at bow hunting. Bow blinds or hides, as they are called, are set up on water holes as an ambush. The blind will usually be at or below ground level. When you are standing in it looking out the window, you are about waist high with the ground. As the animals come in for a drink, you are very close. A lot of the time, you will be in the fifteen—to twenty-yard range. The water hole, if man-made, will usually be designed running lengthwise from you or at a V-shaped angle. This makes the animals stand broadside to you, allowing for a shot when they comes in for a drink. If it's not man-made, there may be logs or other debris strategically placed to get the same broadside effect.

Early-season bow hunting is not a good idea. As bow hunting is done primarily over water holes. There are large amounts of rains that tend to come prior to the early season. Due to that there are numerous amounts of water holes scattered around. This gives the animals a good selection of places to drink. So with that being said, the water hole that you sit on may not get the traffic that you would expect or want.

Later in the season, as things start to dry up, the animals will start to concentrate on the last remaining water holes. Since most areas won't see any significant rain for several months. Now your odds start to go up.

Bow stalking is another method of hunting. This may be an option during the first season with so much of the green bush to hide within. With any bow hunt, the success rate is low, but trying to stalk an African animal is even tougher. Take into consideration that these animals live with some of the most cunning predators around. That makes them extremely wary. Some PHs may not even offer the bow stalk as a hunting option due to the very low chances of pulling it off.

One more thought I should point out on bow hunting. The biggest single thing that deters me from bow hunting in Africa is this: You will spend a considerable amount of money to make this trip happen. When bow hunting, you will crawl into your blind in the morning while it is still dark. Then you will sit there most of the day looking through a small, elongated window at a single water hole. It will be the same view all day. Some days you will come in for lunch and some you may take your lunch into the blind with you. You will sit until it gets dark and then crawl out and go back to camp. This is not the way I want to see Africa. Doing a gun hunt, you will be on the move most of the day, covering hundreds and hundreds of acres. You will see some of unique things that you won't see anywhere else.

And then there's rifle hunting. Most safaris are conducted with a rifle in hand. Before going to Africa, you should take the time to shoot off shooting sticks. You can buy a set or make your own. A lot of the shots that you take will be off sticks so you should be comfortable with them. It's really not hard at all to get used to, but it does take a little practice in finding the sweet spot. You'll want to be able to hit the sweet spot between your gun and sticks without thinking about it. Shot opportunities will come quickly so you have to be ready.

While nothing is guaranteed in a true hunting situation, when gun hunting, your success is considerably higher than that with a bow. Spot and stalk are the usual methods for gun hunting. You'll be on the back of a truck driving slowly on the property looking for animals. Once one is spotted, you'll bail off the truck and start stalking him. It is considered by most unethical to shoot off of the back of the truck. There's a great amount of satisfaction associated with taking your animal after a stalk. You will know that you honestly worked for it.

Chapter 10

Taxidermy: US versus Africa

A young female nyala.

Many months before your safari begins, you should have taken the time to decide on taxidermy. You have a couple of options. Get your trophies mounted in Africa or the US. The taxidermy will be one of the major expenses of your trip, so do some research and figure out the best way to get it done.

Let's take a look at African mounted. The taxidermists in South Africa are mounting impala, gemsbok, zebra, and the like every day. They can do them in their sleep. If there is a problem with something on your cape or skin, they can readily replace it if it comes down to that. They will have access to more references for the trophies that they mount than most US taxidermist, being that they are in the country where they are found. That's not to say that the US taxidermist can't do a great job because they certainly can. Having your trophies mounted in Africa will usually be cheaper. Prices tend to be more reasonable across the board with all species on the African side. Going the SA route, you will have to send pictures via e-mail explaining exactly how you want things mounted. I would send several examples of what I was looking for. I would even go as far as to send a picture of the wall or floor space where the mount is going. This will give them a clearer picture of what you want. If it were a detailed mount, I would also expect to get updated photos from them as things are progressing. Be specific with what you want. I have seen people shoot animals and just say, "Make it a shoulder mount." Not mentioning whether it's head up or down left or right. Then complain when they get their animals from the taxidermist and it's not what they wanted. Again it's the details that make or break a trip.

And now let take a look at the US mounted trophies. US mounts also are of excellent quality, but the prices tend to be a bit higher. I may step on some toes here but this is just my opinion. The guys that mount them do a great job but it seems to me that the price for a mount tends to jump about 30 percent when you put the word African in front of the animal's name. If there is a problem with the cape or skin, the US taxidermist are somewhat limited on what they can replace. On the plus side, you can possibly visit the US shop to make sure your mount is exactly as you want it.

You need to compare prices, so you'll need to get quotes from several taxidermists in the US and some from SA. Now this is where your spreadsheet comes in again. Place the names of the animals down the side and the taxidermist across the top. Now you can compare apples to apples. Your totals will be across the bottom. And you'll also need to add in a line for shipping and importation fees.

Shipping cost is something to look into as well. Shipping cost will vary greatly depending on what you have done to your trophies. You have several options to shop. There may be three companies to deal within the shipping process. Your South Africa taxidermist will dip or mount your trophies. Then a shipping company will handle the crated trophies. And then a US importer will take care of the importation process and shipping to you within the states. Ask your taxidermist or PH what shipping companies they use. They should be able to provide you with at least a few. This may also be taken care of and included with your taxidermy quote. If the taxidermist gives you a quote on the taxidermy and shipping, don't accept the first quote on shipping. Ask for additional shipping company names and quotes so you have something to compare it to. Just as you compared outfitters and taxidermist, you should compare shipping cost as well.

Check with a US importer such as Coppersmith on the pricing and procedures for importing sport hunted game. You may have a shipper that ships your trophy to the US, but it will be up to you to take care of the importation process. Other shippers will use an importer and include that cost in your shipping quote.

Although you have two basic options to consider for getting your trophies mounted, I have offered up a third option that is geared for the average guy on a budget.

Option 1: Have your trophies completely mounted in South Africa. This means that when you get your trophies home, all you'll have to do is uncrate them and hang them on the wall. Some of the horns may have to be attached. The mounted animals are shipped with the horns off. They will be wrapped up and padded in the bottom of the crate to take up less space in the crate. Shipping is bill according to the crate size or the weight, whichever one is greater. You can save a lot of money on the taxidermy, but sometimes the shipping will be high due to the large crate of fully mounted trophies. This may be a wash compared to the US mount trophies. You'll just have to compare the two to see which one is most feasible for you.

Option 2: Have them dipped and then shipped. Before any animal is exported to the US, it must be dipped and inspected for parasites or diseases. This is done alone before shipping or as part of the taxidermy process. After this, you would receive them in a much smaller crate than you would if you had them mounted. Once in the US, they would generally go to the tannery for tanning. Your chosen taxidermist may have them sent there directly or shipped to him for his own personal inspection and then on to the tannery. Once the hides are tanned, they would be shipped to your taxidermist for mounting. He then mounts them right here in the US, and either you pick them up and he ships them to you, or he delivers them to you in person.

Option 3: As I said before, this is more for the everyday workingman on a budget that can't afford to get all his animals mounted at once. Let's say you shoot five or six animals. You can have the skinner cape them out for shoulder mounts as well as save the skulls for skull (or European) mounts. You then have the skulls cleaned up and bleached and also have the hides tanned very inexpensively by a South African taxidermist. Once finished, they are shipped directly to you. You can then put the skull mounts on the wall to show everyone what you took on your safari and put away the tanned capes. Now let say three or four months down the road you get enough money to shoulder mount one or two animals. You take the cape and the skull in to your local taxidermist in the US to be mounted. He will cut the horns off the skull and mount your animal with your cape. Then, say, six months later, you save up enough money to mount a couple more and repeat the process until all your animals are mounted. This way, you still get to show off all your animals on display and mount them as you can afford to.

Don't forget taxidermy tags to go on your animals. You need to get tags from your chosen taxidermist to make sure that they go to the proper place. They may be as simple as a business card that's been laminated or placed in a plastic sleeve with a string attached. These tags are in your possession well before you leave on your safari. The tag will have your name, number, and address as well as that of your taxidermist in which the animal is supposed to go to. You will need at least three tags for each animal you plan to shoot but you should try to take five to be on the safe side. One will be attached to the skull or horns, one will be on the cape, and the other for the back skin not used on the mount if you have it tanned for pillows or other novelty items. You may decide to do something with the feet or tail as well. Some PHs may also want to double tag the horns just in case one tag is lost.

What's the time frame for getting trophies home? If you do the dip and ship, you may have your trophies on there to you as soon as three or four months. The tan and ship may be in the six months or so range. Going the complete SA mount and ship will be around twelve to fourteen months give or take. These are only estimated time frames. You need to check with your potential taxidermist on your list to get their estimate on how long things should take.

Shipping your trophies by air versus sea. You have two choices when it comes to shipping your trophies across the water. You should ask for pricing both ways so that you can compare the two options.

Cargo waiting to be loaded into the cargo hold of a jumbo jet.

Option A is if the crate is small enough, you may be able to have your shipment done by air. The taxidermist will dip or mount your trophies. Then they will be crated and sent to the customs' office at the airport in South Africa. Once they have the proper paperwork checked off, they are inspected and loaded on a plane. The length of time will, once shipped, may only be a couple of weeks. After the plane lands in the US, the crate has to go through the Customs and the Fish and Wildlife Departments. Once cleared, it can be forwarded on to you. At this point, you may want to employ the services of an importer. An import broker is a company or person that clears your shipment through Customs and the Fish and Wildlife Departments. They will file the necessary paperwork on your behalf through a power of attorney document that you fill out with them. They can also arrange for the shipping of your crate on its US leg to your home. Although some find it complicated, you may if you choose fill out your own paperwork and do the filings yourself. But remember, the importer does this every day for a living. They will know all the ins and outs of the process.

Option B is by sea. Your crate, depending on its size, may have to be shipped by a cargo ship. Marine freight will almost always be the cheaper way to go in the long run. The drawback is that you have a much longer wait for your delivery. Once the ship leaves the South African port, it will be on the ocean for three weeks. There are multiple ports of entry in the US including Houston or New York. From there, it has to go through Customs and Fish and Wildlife before it can be shipped on by truck to your house. The chances of the crated trophies getting damaged while en route to the US increase when shipped by marine. Although they may be packaged and padded, it's a long eight thousand-plus miles ride to get here. There could be some shifting in the crate caused by rough waters or possibly get water damaged from a strong storm at sea. It's a good idea to look into shipping insurance. The shipping company will be able to give you prices and different rates on this. The crate will be in one of those large shipping containers. Often the shipping container will have mostly or all sport hunted trophies from a number of hunters.

CHAPTER 11

Medicines and Vaccinations

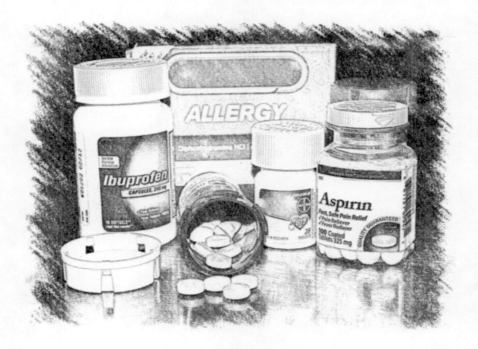

An assortment of medicines to consider packing for safari.

First and foremost, you should consult your own doctor for medicines and vaccinations. A physical checkup is also advisable. I am not in any way giving any medical advice. I am simply stating what I did personally as a precaution. Your private doctor will be able to look up the area you intend to visit and give you the proper vaccines.

Malaria is probably the main concern for most people as it was for me. The first thing I did was go to the CDC or (Center for Disease Control) website and pull up the country and area that I am going to. They will have a list of current health alerts in effect for that specific area. Most areas in SA are malaria free, but I took the pills anyway just as a precaution. I had a choice for pills that you take daily and some that you take weekly. Ask about side effects for the different medications that you will be taking. The last thing you want is to get to South Africa, start a new medication, and then feel bad from the side effects the whole time your there.

Another place to look for help on your medications is your local county health department. They will have some of the harder to find vaccines such as the yellow fever and typhoid vaccines if necessary. If you are going into certain other countries on your South Africa trip, they may require you to have a yellow fever card before entering. This card shows that you have had the shot. Make sure that your tetanus shots are up to date. There will be a good chance of getting scratched in the bush.

For me, a sleep aid from my doctor helped with the transition into the South African time zone. Again I am not recommending you take any medications whatsoever, I am simply telling you what I did. If you don't want to ask your doctor for something, you should, if feasible, start to try to adjust your sleeping habits a few days before you leave. Remember, it's a big time difference between the US and South Africa, so you must make plans for the transition.

When I would normally go to bed at 11:00 PM central time in the US, it would be the same as the time to get up at 6:00 AM in South Africa. So a serious plan had to be devised. For my flight that departed Dulles in DC at 5:20 PM, my plan was to go to sleep as soon as I could on the plane. Around 6:00 to 7:00 PM was my target time. This is where the sleep aids from my doctor came in. My goal was to sleep until about 1:00 AM US central time. That would put me waking up around 7:00 or 8:00 AM on South African time. Then I had to stay awake until it was about 9:00 PM bedtime in South Africa. For me, this method worked seamlessly. I slept that first night and all the others while in South Africa as if I were at home in my own bed.

The time zone change coming home required a little diligent planning as well. For my flight that left at 10:00 PM South African time, I needed to stay awake on the plane until 4:00 to 5:00 AM South African time. That would put me going to sleep at 9:00 to 10:00 PM US central time. Then after about eight hours of sleep I would wake up on US time. I found that the transition back to US time was a little more challenging than the transition from US to South African time.

Your US time zone may be different from the one I'm in, so take the time and do some calculating. It will make the difference between being groggy and sleepy all day when you should be awake on your toes hunting or being wide awake staring at the ceiling at night when you should be sleeping and getting plenty of rest.

Chapter 12

Flight Options to South Africa

An Airbus 340 wide-body jet preparing to be pushed off from the gate.

There are a few of options for arrival times in South Africa. The most popular airline is probably going to be South African Airways. You will have to look at the different arrival times for the flights. The arrival time will determine whether or not you need to plan an overnight stay upon arrival in Johannesburg or if you'll be able to go directly to camp. Most PHs prefer to not drive to camp at night. If you have to overnight in Johannesburg, ask your PH what he would recommend as for as a place to stay. Most likely, you are not the first hunter he as had to have to overnight there, and he probably has something already set up with a hotel or bed and breakfast.

You have a choice of going online and booking your flights yourself or utilizing the services of a booking agent. You will find a lot of great deals online for travel, but the tough part is figuring out which one to choose. Initially, I had planned to book my own flights and save lots of money. I was going to minimize the time I had for layovers to the bare minimum. I was thinking maybe an hour in between flights. That would give me enough time to get to the next gate without having to wait in the terminal for three and a half hours. Sounds like the perfect plan, right? Wrong! I wised up and chose to use a booking agent. Unlike an everyday run-of-the-mill travel agent, a booking agent knows about hunting trips and traveling with guns. While a travel agent can get you into a nice hotel just outside the gate at Magic Kingdom, they may be lacking in the area of the inner workings of the ten-page South Africa Police Service (SAPS) form 520. The true impact of the few dollars that you think you are saving by booking online may not be realized in the beginning. When you are running through the airport like a madman barely missing the only flight of the day to South Africa is when it hits you and you say to yourself, "Wow, I think I screwed up." The booking agent will be up to date on changes in the country that you are going to that may affect your hunt. You will be provided with phone numbers to contact them should something come up. Yes, you can save money by booking flights yourself, but it's usually a very small amount. Most booking agents for hunters know a lot of the PHs and have hunted some of the countries that they are sending you to. There will be agents at the hunter's shows that you can talk to and ask questions.

You should book early to get the best price on your flights. Generally speaking, the earliest that you can book a flight is about 330 days out. You can wait a bit to see if the fares go down, but there is no guarantee that they won't go up at the same time. March, April, and May will be a little easier to book fights as these are not big travel months with the exception of spring break of course. June, July, and August are busy summer travel months to begin with, so if you are looking at a late season hunt, the earlier you book your flight the better off you will be. Most airlines start to raise the price the closer to the departure date that you get.

Take the time to select you seats. The flight to OR Tambo International Airport in Johannesburg will be around seventeen to eighteen hours. You will want to be as comfortable as you can afford. For me, anything other than economy was out of the question due to the price. The price examples that I'll give here are round-trip airfare originating from Dallas, Ft. Worth International Airport to Johannesburg, South Africa.

First class seats will start from $8,000 up round-trip for those who can afford it or may have travel points to cash in. These seats are very comfortable. It will be like sitting in your recliner at home. It will also lay flat like a bed so you can get some rest.

Business class is not for off in price from first class and will be from $6,000–$8,000. These seats are also quite comfortable and will usually boast plenty of connections for your electronics.

And economy seating will be in the $1,700–$1,800 range on the low end. This will vary depending on where your originating flight is the US. The price difference in the upgrade from economy could mean a lot of extra trophies or excursions for your trip.

The seats are not all that roomy if you are a tall person such as myself or a heavyset person. There are emergency exit doors in the cabin of the plane. The seats found on these rows have considerably more legroom. But these seats are usually hard to get. They are mostly saved for the premier or preferred fliers with the airline as a perk. So the chances of upgrading to one of these seats are slim, but it never hurts to ask anyway. My suggestion to you is ask for bulkhead seating. These seats are located behind a wall or bulkhead, and there is ample legroom. The seat configuration on most of the South Africa Airways Airbus 340s is two on the outside, four in the middle, and then two on the other side. So you still have the option of a window or an aisle seat if you get the bulkhead. There is a plus and a minus to consider with these seats. The plus is you are probably going to be right next to the lavatory, so you won't have to walk far to get there. The drawback is there may be a line of people standing in the aisle next to you waiting to use the lavatory for extended periods during the flight.

Prepare your mind-set for a lengthy flight. Stressing out over the length of the flight can ruin your last few days before you depart for your hunt as the dread starts to set in. It can also creep in on you again before you leave South Africa. Just get it in your head that in order to get to South Africa, you have to endure the long flight. Then get over it and focus on the hunt.

I can't speak for the other airlines, but South Africa Airways has individual TV screens for all seats on the Airbus 340 plane. There are movies and TV shows and games that you can play. You should bring plenty of reading material or music if you prefer. Although it is a seventeen—or so-hour flight, you should be sleeping for about eight hours of it. That means you're only awake for eight or nine hours. Looking at it that way helps make the flight a bit more bearable. From the time I departed on my initial flight in the US until the time I touched down in Johannesburg was about twenty-eight hours. You should expect to be in this duration range including layovers.

Chapter 13

A Few Things You Should Consider

The author having an on up-close encounter with a bull elephant just outside of camp.

There are some insurance policies that you should think about. Trip cancellation insurance will cover the cost of your trip should something happen that prevents you from going or having to cut your trip short once there.

There are several different companies that offer trip cancellation insurance. Most outfitters may only refund a small portion of your deposit should you cancel. It usually depends on how far out you cancel before your safari starts. The closer to your departure date, the less likely you are to get a full refund. Outfitters spend a lot of time and money to book clients. There are only so many slots to put clients in for the year. So if you cancel at the last minute, they can't fill your spot. That causes them to lose a sizeable portion of their income. Some may not refund your deposit at all. Ask questions. Trip cancellation insurance would normally cover all the money that you spent on your safari up to the point of cancellation including the deposit if your PH kept it and you did not get it back. Safari Club International members have a trophy insurance available to them. This would cover your unmounted animals while at the taxidermist and once they are mounted and hanging on the wall at your home.

In the event that something unexpected should happen, you may want to think about an insurance policy. You have several other options for insurance. There are emergency medical rescue plans and security evacuation plans.

Most hunters don't think about it, but your US-issued medical insurance will not work for you in South Africa. That's where the emergency medical policy comes in. Should you become ill in a remote location and cannot get to the hospital on your own, you will be rescued from the field. They will use vehicles or aircraft to get to you and transport you out. Additionally, the medical plan may also include assistance with lost medicines, passports, or things of that nature.

The security evacuation plans are for anything nonmedical that would require you to be evacuated. They include things such as war, natural disasters, or terrorist acts.

There are a few of companies that are well-organized in this area. The one I would recommend for medical as well as emergency evacuation is Global Rescue. They have short-term policies that you can purchase for one, two weeks, or a month at a time. They even have yearly and family plans. Having one or both of these plans in place for your safari is not a must, but they are very good ideas. They will give peace of mind to those who are back at home while you are off on your big adventure. If you don't already have one, an accidental death policy is another consideration you should think about.

Now we get into the core of the trip of a lifetime concept, the dollars and sense. As you are starting to see it takes a lot to execute a safari in South Africa so a second trip may be out of the question for many. I'm talking about planning your safari as though you may never go back. Some people think to keep the expenses down and make the first trip a small one and only take two, three, or maybe just four animals. Then maybe a few years later, I'll save up and go get the rest of the animals on my wish list. This sounds good, but let's look at some things you may not have thought of.

Remember, I said that you should plan your hunt for as long as you could possibly afford. Here's why. First is the cost of getting there and your daily rate. This is just the cost of being in camp and being taken care of whether you shoot any animals or not.

As I mentioned before, the round-trip airfare will be in the $1,700 range depending on what part of the country you are traveling from.

Next, let's consider your daily rate. You should expect to pay anywhere from $375 up for a first-time hunt. If you stay in that range, you will find an outfitter that will give you the experience that you are looking for. Drop below $350 per day and you have to question a lot of things. Is this really an all-inclusive deal or am I going to get hammered at the end of the safari for extras. You need to know these things the day you book your safari.

To put things in perspective, to get a good professional hunter will be $150 per day. So when someone offers you a safari for $250 per day, you have to ask yourself, "What am I getting for that?" How is he going to feed you and have a PH with you each day? How is he going to run a vehicle and fill it with diesel every day? And let's not forget about the entire camp staff. They don't work for free. If you are offered a deal that looks too good to be true, you will likely be disappointed in the end when they fail to deliver.

Now we will assume you are on a ten-day hunt. So that's $350 times ten equaling $3,500. Add that to the $1,700 airfare and you have $5,200 invested before you ever pull the trigger. Now you've spent $5,200 to be in South Africa to shoot four animals excluding the cost of the animals. If you decide to make your second trip a few years down the road you should expect a slight price increase over that. So your second trip will cost you at least $5,200 again for another four animals. Going with two small trips will cost you over ten thousand dollars to shoot eight animals Instead, if need be, save another year or two to and spend that $5,200 on more animals or maybe an excursion on your first trip. You have to maximize you dollars by shooting as many animals as you can afford on this first trip. If you can swing a second trip, all the better but plan as though you may never go back!

The cost of shipping will be more cost effective in one shipment versus two. Remember, the shippers will bill you by either weight or volume of the crate, whichever is greater. But there are still the base costs involved in getting your animals home. So it will be more cost effective to get it all done on one trip.

Your physical condition matters in the bush. You should consult with your doctor or physician before starting an exercise program.

Your hunting experience will be greatly enhanced by the shape you're in. I'm not saying that you should be able to run a marathon or climb a mountain. But you will want to be able to keep up with your PH when on the trail of an animal. This is not to say that the PH won't adjust his pace for you because he will. I understand that everyone's physical ability is not at the same level, but you should be in the best shape you can be in for your hunt. It would be a shame to see the trophy animal of your dreams and not be able to get to a position to take him because you're exhausted and out of breath, all because you didn't take the time to get a little exercise before you came to hunt. It could be as simple as taking a walk every day. But again check with your doctor before starting.

Communicating with the world back home. There may or may not be Internet in camp. In those instances, a satellite phone may be the answer. A satellite phone, as they are called, can keep you connected. You'll be able to call home every day for a couple minutes if you wanted or needed to or utilize it in an emergency situation in the field. There is a lot to be said for hearing a loved one's voice when you're eight thousand miles away. They work a lot like a cellular phone, but instead of towers, they link with satellites orbiting the Earth. All you need is a clear view of the sky. You can buy a block of airtime or pay by the minute depending on how much you plan to use it. There are a variety of different optional accessories available from data texting to Internet. I have rented sat phones from Explorer Satellite Com. in Florida. Currently they are renting them for about $85 to $100 per week plus about $2 a minute.

The process is fairly simple. You tell them where you are going and when you need the phone. They will ship it right to your doorstep and you ship it back to them when you get back home. Your outfitter will sometimes have a satellite phone that you can use. He may charge you about five dollars per minute but you won't have to pay a rental fee.

I think that that the most economical means of communicating back home is texting. If you can get a cellular signal in camp, you might want to purchase an international data plan through your carrier. The cellular coverage areas are amazing in South Africa. Even in some of the more remote areas. Be sure and ask your outfitter if you have access in camp.

Going back to the observer on you safari. Observers are great if they are your best friend that you get along with great or your wife. When it comes to your wife, you must be under no illusion of what being on a safari means. With this, I mean that if she is someone that doesn't like nature, if she is someone that doesn't like insects, if she is someone that doesn't like dirt and thorns or if she doesn't like a combination of all these, you must make it very, very clear to her this is what she is going to do.

Give her an idea of what her day will be like because it will not be very different from yours unless she is staying in camp. If it's in the early or late season, there will likely be a swimming pool in camp that she can enjoy. She must know that it's your hunting trip. If she is a mall girl or a five-star hotel girl, you will not enjoy your safari. She will want to come home every single day. Don't take this the wrong way, but you must explain everything properly. We are going to Africa. We are going to be in the bushes. There are no malls. There are no movies, and there is no jewelry. None of that exist until we get back to town. If she is all right with following you around in the bush or sitting in camp not doing much, by all means, bring her along. If that is not her cup of tea, don't put yourselves in that situation. If you do, your troubles will start the day you arrive in Africa and will end thirty years later. Don't try to sell your safari to her in the hopes that she will agree just because she's going along also. Let her know here's the trip and you would love for you to go with you. But you should be clear on the fact that it is a hunting trip.

CHAPTER 14

Guns for Africa

Keeping the rifles handy during a midmorning break.

There has been a lot of talk and books on the subject of safari rifle. While there are minimum caliber requirements, I think it really boils down to your own personal preference. Most deer rifles will do the job for plains game. It doesn't do any good for you to take a big gun that kicks like a mule if you're going to flinch every time you squeeze the trigger. You won't hit your mark and will end up paying for a wounded animal that you couldn't recover.

What are the calibers to consider? Personally I am very comfortable with shooting my .270 Ruger, but it is the minimum size that you would want to take on a safari. Some other calibers that will work for plains game are the 7mm, 30.06, .300 win mag., and .308. One of the .300 calibers would do very well for most of the plains game species. The bigger calibers such a .375 are what you should consider if you will be hunting larger game like giraffe or eland. If you want to do a one-gun safari, get one of the .300 calibers with a 180 grain round will work on small antelope and the bigger ones as well.

But if you don't have one of the larger caliber guns, don't worry. Before you go out and buy another gun just to shoot one or two animals, talk to your PH. He most likely will have something you can rent or borrow for your hunt. The cost for renting a gun can vary starting from $20 a day plus ammo to simply borrowing the gun and paying for the ammo you use. It may not feel like your gun, but it will still get the job done.

Whatever you borrow from the outfitter is supplied at a cost to him. If you ask to shoot birds and only shoot ten rounds out of the box, don't offer to pay for the ten. Offer to pay for the whole box. Ammunition in South Africa is considerably more expensive than in the States. So don't nitpick on the little things. It only creates tension at the end of the day, and it's just the right thing to do.

Taking time at the rifle range on the first day in camp to make sure the scope is still on.

What are the scopes to consider for Africa? Super high-powered scopes are not totally necessary. Most of your shots are going to be around 150-to 200-yard range. You need one that gives you enough light for a clear sight picture of your target. Three by nine is a good choice. Magnification over twelve power is good, but the slightest movements while fully zoomed in will show a lot of exaggerated movement in the sight picture. Six power is usually all that will be used in most plains game situations.

PH Paul Stones suggests that if you are going to buy a rifle and scope, you should put more emphasis on the scope. Buy yourself a good rifle that will shoot well. Then put on an upper-end scope. At the end of the day, it's the scope that will make or break your safari as far as your shots are concerned.

Binoculars for safari can vary. I personally like the 10×26 size, but I have found them a little small when sitting on a ridge doing some serious glassing from a ridge top. The binoculars for safari should be at least 10×30. Bigger can be better, but they will become cumbersome and in the way while stalking. You will want to make sure they have lens that won't fog up when you look through them. But with that being said, you won't be relying on your binoculars all that much. Most of you views of the animals you're after will be through your riflescope. Things can happen fast in the bush. So when you're on the trail of an animal and your PH says there he is at 125 yards, you should be reaching for your gun, not your binoculars.

What's the number of rounds to take? Sixty rounds of good 150–180 grain ammunition should be sufficient. My personal preference is the Federal Premium Nosler Partition. I've had great success with this bullet in the 150 grain in my .270. I know most everyone has his or her own preference when it comes to ammunition. Just make sure you get as heavy a grain bullet as you can accurately shoot from your gun. Most African animals are tough and need a good penetrating bullet to take them down. Also remember to sight your gun in with the same ammo that you will be shooting on your hunt. Some people will try to sight their guns in with cheap ammo and save the good stuff for the hunt. You must sight it in with the same ammo that you will be hunting with. Different brands as well as different types of the same brand will travel differently from your gun. A bad shot wounding and losing a $1,600 animal is a hard is a hard lesson learned.

The ammo will need to be in its original box and then placed inside a lockable box. A small plastic gun box will work. The total weight should not exceed eleven pounds. You should purchase Transportation Security Administration (TSA) locks to go on your ammo box. A TSA lock has this TSA symbol on it. It will also have a number that the agent will match to his master keys to open your lock without having to have you present. Place your locked ammo box in your checked luggage, not your carryon bags. Placing it in the top of your bag will help the TSA agents have easier access to it should they want to examine it closer. That way, they won't have to dig through all of your carefully packed belongings.

What type of gun cases should you use? The case that you take your gun to Africa in should be of good quality. It will serve you no purpose to purchase a cheap gun case and risk damage to your gun during transport in the cargo hold of the airplane. Luggage handlers are notoriously rough on the bags they handle. There are a variety of cases to choose from. Most are the coffin-hinged design. Other popular models are built like a golf bag in which the guns are loaded from the top. The model I have is a double gun case. The centerpiece comes out so you can place one gun in the bottom and then the other goes on the top. If you are hunting with a buddy, one double case will take care of both of your guns. Remember, your gun case counts as one of your checked bags on the airline, so doubling up gives you an extra bag if you need it. Even if you only take one gun with you I would still recommend a double case. You can store your binoculars, knives, or other security sensitive things in the extra space. The weight of your case will still come under the microscope so to speak. The heavy metal cases don't leave much leeway when it comes to the fifty-pound limit. A plastic case like this one weighs twenty pounds empty and about forty pounds with two guns and a few accessories in it. For your trip on the plane, your gun should be in your case unloaded and with the bolt out if it's a bolt-action gun. And again, your ammo cannot be in the same case as your gun. It should be in a locked case in your checked luggage. All ammunition must be of the same caliber. This means, for example, if you are hunting with a .270, you cannot bring a box of .375 rounds for the PHs gun that you plan to use.

Someplace in your bags, try to fit in a soft gun case. You will need a soft case for your gun while on the back of the truck. It should be one that's light but preferably padded. The roads can be rough and are very dusty during the dry season in South Africa so you might want to also pack a gun cleaning kit. At the very least, you should take along some lens cleaning cloths.

TSA locks are something that you must have on your gun case. They may be the padlock type or they may be made into the case such as the ones I have here. Again, the lock will have a number on it that the TSA agent will use to match that lock with the proper passkey. If there is not a TSA lock, they will have to page you in the airport to come and unlock it for them. This raises an unwanted red flag that may subject you and your case to a more stringent inspection. Not to mention the risk of making you late or missing your flight altogether. And remember; keep your keys handy just in case you do need to unlock it for them.

There is one other thing you should know. You cannot take two guns of the same caliber under the same name to South Africa. By this, I mean, let's say you own two .270 rifles. You plan on using one and your son or wife will be hunting with the other. You will not be able to import them both in your name. The same would apply to two twelve-gauge shotguns. If you are planning on doing some wing shooting, there is a special permit that may be obtained for shotguns. If you arrive in South Africa with two rifles of the same caliber in your name, the South African airport police will take one of them. It will be returned to you upon our departure out of the country. And since we are on the subject, you cannot bring ammunition for your PHs gun in which you plan to use.

Chapter 15

Customs Forms and Rifle Permit

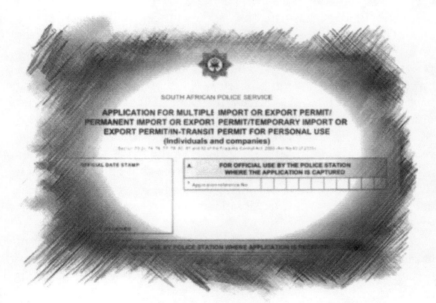

The ten-page SAPS 520 form that is required to import your rifle into South Africa.

Filling out your customs form is not all that difficult. And as for the rifle importation papers, you can do it yourself or use a rifle permit company. First, we'll go over the customs form.

US Customs Form 4457 is a form that you must acquire prior to your departure. You must take your firearm to a US Customs office and register it with them prior to leaving the country. It is a simple form that verifies with a seal the serial numbers and that you are the owner of the weapon. If you try to bring your weapon back into the US without this form, it is considered a felony for gun trafficking and you may be arrested. Also it is illegal to take your gun hunting and then leave your firearm in South Africa. It is a good idea to get this form at least six months before your safari date just in case there is a problem. Other items that you are taking such as rangefinders, jewelry, still and video cameras, laptop computers, etc. should also be taken to the customs office and listed on the form. Their serial numbers will also be verified on the form proving that you did in fact leave the country with the items. Sales receipt or registration papers may be accepted for some personal items. Otherwise, you'll run the risk having to pay a duty tax on your own property upon your return. Most of the major airports will have a customs office. This is a lifetime document that can be used for future trips.

If you are planning to take your own gun, you should familiarize yourself with the South Africa Police Service or SAPS form 520. This is a ten-page form that is required to take your gun on safari in South Africa. The good news is that not every single line needs to be filled out in it's entirety. You can download and print out the form from the SAPS website. There are instructions along with the form. Take your time on this form and fill it out carefully. There are the stories of hunters spending hours in line in South Africa with forms in hand only to have to fill out the form again because something was not filled out correctly.

I have used the services of a company called Riflepermits.com. You will be met at the airport and led to the SAPS office where they will finalize your papers. They have on their website the necessary instructions to fill the form out. Then you scan and e-mail a copy of the finished form to them for verification. Once approved, you mail or currier the originals along with a copy of your passport, travel itinerary, Customs form 4457, and an invitation letter from you outfitter. The invitation letter is one that basically states that you are going to South

Africa to hunt with ABC Company from this date to this date. Your PH will provide this along with the questionnaire once you have booked your hunt. If you are traveling during the late season with a gun, things may get a little more hectic. It could take you a few hours doing your paperwork on your own depending on how many hunters arrive in the airport around the same time as you. I've also heard hunters say that they didn't have any problems at all. With the help of Riflepermits.com and the current cost of $90, I was out within ten to fifteen minutes. With their services, my permit was approved prior to my arrival. It's really a personal call on your part on whether or not to spend the money.

CHAPTER 16

Proper Shot Placement on African Animals

An old African cape buffalo bull that has been separated from the main herd; also known as dugga boy.

Making a good first shot is very important. Most African animals have their vital organs more forward in the chest than the ones in North America. For this reason, you should learn where to shoot them. There are several shot placement posters and books out there. I recommend you get a pocket version. This small booklet will fit into a shirt pocket for looking over while you are on the plane, in camp, or as a quick reference just before leaving the truck and making a stalk. It gives you diagrams of where the organs are positioned depending on whether the animal is quartering toward you, quartering away, facing you head on, and so on.

I'm sure you've noticed that I have mentioned this several times already. I can't stress this enough. Make sure you make the shot count!

Some of you are sitting there saying I've shot a dozen or so deer over the years with no problem. While that may be true, safari hunting is a bit different. When you shot your deer, you were probably sitting in a blind with a steady rest in a comfortable chair. When on a safari, you will likely jump out of the truck after spotting your prize or you may be on foot walking. Then you might have to make a run for a clear shooting lane and then drop your barrel down on the shooting sticks. At this point, you may be out of breath, and you may only have five to ten seconds to make a good shot on a $1,200 animal. I'll say this twice so that I get your attention. If you wound him, you bought him whether he's recovered or not. If you wound him, you bought him whether he's recovered or not. You have to trust the people you are with to make a judgment call. There are certain shots that are fired and there is no doubt in the mind of the PH, the tracker, and yourself that the animal was indeed hit. However, as you move forward to the spot where it stood, and the trackers find no blood. Finding no blood does not constitute a miss. There are shots that are clearly hits based solely on the reaction of the animal. Most cases you will find blood. You knew when you shot whether it felt like a hit or miss. If the animal leaps six feet into the air, there's no question about it. For every animal that's hit, it must be reported to the outfitter as well as the landowner because now there is money involved. And that is why I say to be in the best physical shape as you can.

Planning An African Safari

Another four-mile hiking day on the tracks of the elusive eland.

This brings me to another point. You should always be ready to shoot in the bush. I'm not at all saying that you should have your finger on the trigger while walking. You could sling your gun on your shoulder but try not to get too comfortable with it. You should be able to bring your gun up to a shooting position fairly quickly. Personally, I prefer not to hunt with a sling on my gun. I like to have it in my hands at all times. The strap tends to get in the way when I'm trying to settle into the sweet spot on the shooting sticks. You should not carry your rifle over your shoulder in the traditional African fashion with your hand on the barrel. It is very dangerous as your PH and trackers will be in front of you. Your barrel will swing across them all day. It's a good idea to practice shooting from different positions. Lying prone, standing free or off-hand, kneeling, and even sitting. Some of the more expert shots recommend practicing with your opposite shooting hand for that tricky shot that you otherwise couldn't get in position for.

You should not shoot until told to do so by your PH. You may think you're on the right animal, but he is looking at something else. He may see a broken horn tip or other flaw that you don't. The bottom line is, the PH calls the shots.

Only shoot ranges that you are comfortable with. Most shots will be two hundred yards or less. Most of those falling in the 125–150 yard range. There may be the odd two hundred–yard plus shot, but remember, you wound it, you pay for it—whether it's recovered or not. If you are not comfortable with the distance, tell the PH you need to try to get closer. He will do what he can to close the distance for you. You're paying the bill, so taking the shot is always on your final call.

CHAPTER 17

What Do You Need to Pack for Your Safari?

You should take the things that will make you trip comfortable, but don't overpack.

Suitcase weight is something you need to be conscientious of. To avoid the extra baggage fees for most airlines, you need to stay under fifty pounds. With that being said, don't pack your bags at home at forty-nine pounds. If you plan on bringing back any souvenirs, you'll be overweight. You may also want to consider taking an extra duffel bag folded up in your luggage just for souvenirs. Most airlines allow one carry-on suitcase and one small bag. If you buy something fragile, put it in the duffel bag and take it as a carry-on bag. Some airlines have started charging a fee for checked luggage, and they usually allow two pieces. Your gun case will count as one of those pieces, and the rest of your hunting gear will be in the other.

Most all camps have a daily laundry service available for the hunters. There is no need to pack an excessive amount of clothes. Some of the things you should have are as follows:

Three changes of hunting clothes will be enough. By the second day, you'll be in a clean set and have a dirty set being washed. You will still have a clean set you will wear on day 3 if your first set is not returned to you yet or you need to change in the middle of the day for some reason.

Note that it is illegal to wear camouflage clothes in some African cities. I should be OK if you are hunting in the bush. So unless I was bow hunting, I would not even take camouflage. Most hunters prefer to wear traditional khaki safari clothing. These are not the very light colors but the ones that are a little bit darker. Pale greens, browns, and grays are the norm in this area. This may be a once-in-a-lifetime trip so you'll want to look your best for the videos and photos that you take. Safari hunting is a very special and memorable journey that very few people get to experience. You posing beside a majestic kudu in a ratty old torn camouflage t-shirt may not be the photo you'll want to be showing off to the grandkids in twenty years.

Comfortable, lightweight, and quiet soles are the main things to look for in a boot. Waterproofing is not a bad idea either. It's best to take two pairs of hunting boots. For me, it's good to give my feet a break of not having to wear the same boots every single day. Or just in case one pair gets wet and needs to dry out. Make sure you break them in well before your hunt. Even with that you should bring plenty of band-aids just in case you do get blisters. Good wool socks will make you daily treks a lot more comfortable. Do not bring sneakers for hunting. They are not designed for the rugged terrain.

A coat that has a zip outliner would be a plus. As I said before, in the mornings it can be pretty cool. So a jacket that you can strip down will benefit you. Otherwise I would take a heavy coat and a light jacket.

You could probably get by with one pair of gloves. I prefer a thin pair. They help in the mornings to cut the chill in the air, but they are not so thick that I can't wear them and shoot my gun. These are also the same type of gloves I would wear while bow hunting.

You'll need something comfortable to wear around camp in the evenings. Warm-ups and sneakers fit the bill for most. It's really up to you and what makes you comfortable.

South Africa is 220 volts, and your US plugs will not work there. A power converter is a must. I have found that the small three-pronged converter that you find in Walmart may not work in South Africa even though it says it will. I discovered a larger converter in a gift shop while in South Africa that works. If you have multiple items that need to be charged or run together at the same time, you may be able to get by with a power strip plugged into the converter. But be careful not to overload it. Without the right converter, you will short out and fry your electronic device. You may also be able to find adapters in the travel or sometimes the camping sections of outdoor stores. You can also just wait and pick up one at the airport upon your arrival.

A flashlight will come in handy around camp and in the field. Something small to medium-sized will do the trick. Don't forget to bring extra batteries or charger for it.

Digital cameras are perfect for safari. You can get hundreds or well over a thousand photos on a single memory card. But take an extra memory card just in case. Take all the pictures you want and worry about deleting the one that are bad or out of focus while back in camp or just wait until you get home. The higher the megapixel camera you have, the better photos you will get. If you're just going to print out four by six album size five or six megapixels will be OK. But if you are planning to have a few enlarged to put in a large frame, an eight-megapixel or higher will be what you want. Just as a backup you might grab one of those cheap disposable cameras and put it in a separate bag just in case your digital camera gets lost or broken.

Video cameras are also great to capture the moments as they unfold. But unless you have someone dedicated to just video only during the hunt it will be very difficult to hunt and video. Don't expect the trackers to help you out. A lot of the trackers don't know how to properly run the camera, and your PH is busy doing his job making sure you're on the right animal. The shows that you see on TV are not easy to make. It takes them days or weeks for everyone and everything including the animal to be in position to get the right angles for the video shot. But don't let this discourage you. You will still be able to get a lot of great footage during the course of your hunt. It will be very dusty on the back of the truck, so keep your cameras in a dust-proof case.

Bring plenty of extra batteries with you. They will add a lot of extra weight on the way over, but you will be that much lighter on the way back. Rechargeable are a good way to go. Just make sure you have batteries in the camera or device and a fresh set with you and ready to go while in the field. Charge them up nightly. A battery charger that is connectable to an auto cigarette lighter socket will keep your batteries charged and close to you during the day. It can break your heart to have your camera batteries die out when you are trying to take a photo of a once-in-a-lifetime moment or an amazing African sunset.

Other smaller items that you'll want to put on a list will be any medications you need to take daily or weekly. You might want to bring a few extra doses just in case your trip is delayed by a few days in some way. Always pack some travel snacks. The airport vending can add up quickly. Don't forget to take your hat and sun block with an SPF 30 will help protect you from the unrelenting African sun, an extra pair of reading glasses or sunglasses, and your personal toiletries. If you decide to take your hunting knife, you should put it in your gun case. You'll need a good waterproof day bag or backpack to take with you on the truck each day.

CHAPTER 18

Your Arrival in the Country

Highway signs in South Africa.

Safety is on the top of everyone's list when traveling abroad. So by being prepared, you will alleviate a lot of the fears. Don't carry large sums of cash if you don't have to stay with your party. Making sure your luggage is packed within the regulations will help with a smooth trip through customs. Don't be surprised if your things are checked by security, that's why we allowed the extra time during our trip. There are usually maps of the airport onboard the plane that you can look over to help get from point the arrival gate to the SAP office.

Once off the plane, you will follow though the corridors to the customs agent area. You should have you passport ready for them to stamp. They may ask you how long you are planning to be in country or what's your business in South Africa.

Once through customs, proceed to the luggage claim area. It's best to get one of the carts as you enter and wait near the carrousel for your bags. Note that your gun will need to be dropped at the next check station to be inspected by the SAP. They will keep your gun until you get to the SAP office and provide the proper paperwork.

From here, you will enter the general meeting area. If you are being met at the airport by your PH, he will be in the general meeting area. There will be maybe a dozen or so people waiting there to pick someone up just like you. If your PH has another person picking you up, they will be holding up a sign with your name on it. Also if you chose to use a company to expedite your rifle permit papers, they will have a sign as well.

If you didn't take your own gun, the PH will take your luggage and you will exit to the parking area and then it's off to camp. If you do have a gun, you will walk around to the SAP office and wait for your turn to have your gun inspected. They will verify that the serial numbers on the gun match the SAP's 520 and the papers are then processed. Depending on how many people are there will determine how long you'll be in line. You could be there for a few minutes or hours. As I mentioned before, with the help of a rifle permit company, I was in and out in less than fifteen minutes. By having been preapproved it seemed like we went straight to the front of the line. The person from the permit company had done this so many times they knew the SAP officer by name.

A morning arrival may mean that you are probably going from the airport straight to camp. But a late afternoon or evening arriving flight might mean an overnight stay in Johannesburg. If you are overnighting in Johannesburg, your PH may have a transfer services to take you from the airport to your hotel or bed and breakfast. He will then come and pick you up in the morning and take you to camp. Again, this is one of the things that you have to decide when you are booking your hunt and flight so that you know your arrival time and can make a proper plan.

CHAPTER 19

What to Expect in Camp

Several individual chalets conveniently arranged around one
main camp house.

Upon arrival in camp, you'll most likely be met and welcomed by the camp staff. They will greet you and help take all of your bags to your room or chalet. There will be a brief tour of the camp and then take a while to get settled in. You'll probably have lunch or dinner then relax a bit and maybe check the site on your gun. If you get to camp early enough, you may have enough light to go hunting that afternoon.

Camp setup can vary from outfitter to outfitter. Some may be purposely put crudely together while others are five stars. To simplify things, there are basically two types of camps—tented and lodge style.

Tented will likely be in the more remote areas, usually a dangerous game type hunt. The outfitter will have everything that will be set up prior to your arrival. For those who truly want to rough it, the tented hunt may fit the bill. For most others, being in midst of all the wild things that go bump in the night may cause for some lost sleep.

Lodge-style hunting is just as the name suggests. In the more luxury style camps, it may be one large lodge with rooms around the perimeter. More rustic settings will have the small individual rooms with individual toilets and showers with hot and cold running water. There will be a main house where some of the meals are taken. Most will offer some type of under-the-stars dining for your evening diner. There is a lot to be said in having your meal while sitting around a campfire listening to the sounds of the African night.

There are three basic hunting methods when it comes to safari hunting. Most PHs have a particular method that they are comfortable with. Some days will be a combination of them all. It will really depend on the layout of the landscape.

Method 1 is sitting in blinds on water holes. If you are bow hunting, water hole blinds will be your main method of hunting as I mentioned earlier. Be sure and ask about this method with your PH. Some outfitters do not allow hunting over the water holes and don't consider it to be fair-chase hunting. The animals should be allowed to safely drink without the fear of ambush by a hunter.

Planning An African Safari

The author getting the location on a kudu bull before starting the hike down the ridge.

A second method is glassing from an elevated perch. If the property lends itself with hill or kopies as they are called, you may spend the first hour or so of your morning and afternoon hunts climbing to the top and glassing for game. From this high vantage point, you can scan for miles in the valley floor below. Here is another instance where being in the best physical shape you can be will pay off. If something is spotted, you may start your stalk from right there off the top of the ridge.

And the third hunting style is spot and stalk off truck. This is the most popular method of safari hunting. It's simply cruising around looking for game. If you see an animal worth taking, your PH will stop the truck and begin the stalk. Again it is considered unethical and in some countries illegal to shoot off of the back of the truck. Additionally, you never load your rifle until you are off of the truck and are in pursuit of an animal. Once back to the truck, you will then unload your gun prior to getting back on the truck.

The hours of hunting will be from daylight to dusk in most cases. Although there are some game reserves that do not allow any hunting after four in the afternoon. This gives you time to find a wounded animal before it gets dark. Otherwise, someone could find themselves in a dangerous situation during the hours after dark. A wounded gemsbok looking to exact revenge could easily injure or kill an unsuspecting person out for an evening walk.

Chapter 20

A Typical Hunting Day

A typical setup for a safari vehicle complete with a wench on the front bumper.

Wake up call will be around 5:30–6:00 am. You are given about a half hour to get up and get dressed before heading over to the main house for breakfast.

Breakfast will vary from something really light to a full platter. Most of the time it will be on the lighter side, for example, toast, cereal, eggs, bacon, or orange juice. The outfitter questionnaire that I mentioned earlier should have listed any special dietary requests that you have.

After breakfast, it's time to get ready to head out. You will need to grab your gun and day bag with your cameras, extra ammo, sun block, ChapStick, and anything else you think you might need and climb onto the truck. If you haven't already done so on the first day of arrival, you will head on over to the gun range. It will surprise you how easy it is for a scope to get bumped off the mark. The luggage handlers are brutal on the bags they handle. This is why you need a good gun case to put your gun in for the trip.

On a typical hunting day after the gun has been sighted in, you will be on the truck by 7:00 AM. The PH may have one of the trackers drive for him and he will sit in the back of the truck with you. He should have an area already in his mind on where the animals that are on the top of your list may be found. Speaking of animals on your list, you should have two lists of desired animals. List A is for the animals that are the most important to you. For example, kudu as your most desired and then followed by a zebra, gemsbok, and warthog. List B may be springbuck, waterbuck, and impala. This helps you to prioritize what you are after. As kudu and zebra are tough hunts you will be after them from the first moment of hunting. If along the way you see a gemsbok or warthog, you'll switch gears and put a stalk on them. Toward the end of your hunt, if you haven't taken all the animals on your A list or if you've completed you're A list, you look at what's on your B list as substitutes.

Sometime around 9:00 or 10:00 AM, your PH may stop for a midmorning break. It could be as simple as just stopping the truck in a clearing and having a snack or it could be more elaborate. It may be chairs set up with a small table, drinks, and finger sandwiches.

You'll head back to camp for lunch at about eleven o'clock. Lunch will be from somewhere around twelve. It may consist of a mixture of domestic beef, chicken or pork, and wild game taken prior to your hunt for the first days or so. After the first few days in camp, the animals that you shoot while there on your hunt may be on the menu. The midday hours are around the time the animals are less active. So you will have the opportunity to get a nap and rest up or explore some of the sights or other interesting things found around camp. I would suggest that you take a journal with you and use this time to write in it. Those little details that may be vivid in your mind at that moment will become fuzzier and fuzzier over time. A journal will help you years down the road to reflect back on and relive those days.

After your midday break, it's back on the truck at two thirty or three o'clock. Again, you'll slowly troll the roads looking for game. This will go on until you find an animal or it starts to get dark.

Once back in camp for the evening, you will have time to clean up and relax around the campfire. Light snacks are set out for the hunters, and now's the time for a drink if you so desire. At 6:30 PM-ish you will enjoy a traditional African diner under the stars recapping the day's events and sharing stories with each other until your ready to retire to your room.

Chapter 21

After the Animal Is Down

The author watches as the PH and trackers clean up
and pose his springbuck for photos.

The hunting shows on TV show you bits and pieces of the hunt. They show you the stalk, the shot, and then the animal lying on the ground with the hunter posing for photos. What goes on in between all these events? Well, let me break it down for you.

Once the animal is shot and tracked down if necessary, he is confirmed dead by touching his eye. Animals die with their eyes open. If you walk up and his eyes are closed, look out. Many a hunter has been injured or worse by animals that they though were dead. After confirmation of death, he will be dragged into a sunny spot or more scenic area. It needs to have the sun in the hunter's eyes and face. This is where you get your good quality photos. The trackers will then cut the weeds from in front of the animal and roll him onto his stomach. Sticks may be used to hold the head in the proper position. Jugs of water will be used to wash the blood off the mouth or wounds to make him more presentable. The hunter takes his position on the ground behind his hard-won prize and smiles for the camera.

This beautiful trophy impala was taken on the last day of my first safari.

Sometimes either you or the PH will do a brief narration if you are shooting video. This brief synopsis of the hunt is to recount the event as they unfolded in the taking of the animal. The events leading up to the spotting of the animal, the stalking, and problems or obstacles you had to overcome in the process of getting in position to make your shot. If you have an idea for a photo that you've seen in a magazine, let your PH know. Tell him, "I would like to sit here" or "Can we place the animal like this?" Not all PHs will tell you where to sit so you should have an idea of what you would like. You should take your time here with your animal and savor the moments. Once you drop him off with the skinner, you won't see it again until it's mounted and shipped to you possibly a year later.

After all the photos are done, the animal is loaded in the truck. The smaller ones are just picked up by a couple of guys, but the larger animals require a bit more muscle. That is where the winch on the front bumper comes into play. The cable is pulled up over the cab and across a pulley that's just behind the cab. It's wrapped around the horns and he is winched up over the tailgate and into the bed of the truck. Usually a simple operation and you're on your way to the skinning shed. But keep your eyes peeled, the hunt is still in progress and you may still have an opportunity at something else.

The tagging of your trophy animal will take place in the skinning area. Upon arrival at the skinners' shed, your animal will be documented in the outfitter's logbook and measurements will be taken. As I mentioned before, the skull with the horns still attached, cape, and back skin will all be tagged all with your name on them. This will be the last that you see of him until he's mounted and at your home.

The skinning shed will most likely have a ceiling hoist for unloading and for hanging the animals while the skinner works on them. Somewhere close by will be a refrigerated cooler to place the meat once the animal has been processed. Most likely it will be a walk-in cooler. Some of the finer cuts of meat will be taken to the camp cook. At some point, after they have been aged a bit, he will prepare a meal with the animal that you shot. The next questions on a lot of people's minds are, "Can I bring my meat home?" The answer to this question is no. The USDA has strict regulations against bringing any wild game or other meat into the country without being licensed to do so. The rest of the meat will hang until it is utilized by the camp or packaged for sale or donated to the needy in certain areas. Nothing is wasted in Africa!

The salt room is the last stop for your animal in camp. This room will have a floor that is sometimes covered a foot deep in salt. Here, the hides are coated in salt to draw out all the moisture and thus slow down the spoiling process. The skulls and horns will be buried in the salt as well. They will stay here until they are delivered to or picked up by the taxidermist for further processing.

CHAPTER 22

Care of Your Trophies

At the skinning shed, an expert skinner capes out a kudu bull before it goes into the salt.

Trophy preparation is very, very important. If your trophy preparation in the bush is not done correctly, your trophy on the wall will not look like it should years later. You have to make sure that your outfitter is on the ball with.

If your animals are being dipped and sent on to you, they will have to be treated. The skins may be soaked for twenty-four hours or more in a pickling solution. This is done in order to kill any bacteria, parasites, or other living organisms that may be present. A second treatment is applied to neutralize the effects of the first treatment. Afterward, the skins are coated in salt, folded, and placed on a rack to dry before crating and being shipped. Again this process will be in the three-month range.

When it comes to mounting your animals, the turnaround is a bit longer. They still have to be treated, but now they go into the line up with all the others that are waiting to be mounted. As the work starts, ask your taxidermist to send you photos of the work in progress. This will ensure that you are getting what you want.

After the mounting is complete a plywood crate is custom built just big enough for your trophy animals. Remember, the shipping company will bill you according to the weight or volume of your crate. Whichever is the greater of the two? They will be mounted to the floor and walls turned in various directions to make them fit in as small a space as possible without them touching each other. If you have rugs or back hides tanned, they will be rolled up and wrapped on the floor along with any horns that are detachable from your mounts. When your shipment arrives, be sure to do a detailed inspection of all items in your crate for damage. If there is a problem, contact your taxidermist as well as the shipper immediately. If you purchased shipping insurance you will be able to be compensated for any of the repair work that you may have to have done.

Once the crate is ready to go, the taxidermist will have the shipper collect it. Then upon final inspection, it will be loaded onto the plane or ship and sent on it's way.

If the importation was included in your shipping quote, you won't have to do anything but wait for the delivery truck to show up at your front door. If not, you will need to have worked out the details with an importer such as Coppersmith to handle the last US leg of the shipment.

CHAPTER 23

Activities after the Hunt

A zebra smells trouble at the water hole as a cheetah tries
to sneak in behind them undetected.

A fter your safari is complete, you may want to consider an excursion. I would recommend you plan if possible for a couple of days of sightseeing or other excursion at the end of your safari. Especially if you don't have a long list for your animals or if you think you might finish things up early, you might want to consider it.

A fishing trip to one of Africa's many lake or rivers or even the coast if you are within a reasonable distance would be one to remember. Fishing for tiger fish can be like none other and may get pretty intense at times.

A guided sightseeing trip into some of the cultural areas will give you some insight on the history of the country as well as her people. South Africa is well known to have some of the finest wines country in the world. So a trip to one of the local wineries may be in order for the connoisseurs.

Photo safaris can add to the once-in-a-lifetime experience and can usually be done inexpensively. Just make sure you bring the highest quality camera you can get your hands on. The photos that you take need to last you a lifetime. So try to do it right. I would highly recommend a trip to one of the wildlife parks such as the five-million acre Kruger National Park. I would plan for at least two days if at all possible. You can get some great photo and video opportunities and see things that you thought you would only see on the National Geographic Channel. Let's not forget the many museums that are available. If you are in the Kruger National Park you should stop by the Letaba camp and see their display of some of the biggest elephant tusk in the world.

A group of African children walking home
after a day of studying at school.

Another consideration would be a helicopter or hot-air balloon trip. By air, you will be able to see entire herds of animals as they span across the beautiful African landscape from a whole new perspective. It's truly a breathtaking experience and one that will not soon be forgotten.

The return of a four-seat helicopter flying just over the treetops after a morning game viewing flight.

Chapter 24

It's All about the Money

Start saving right now for your safari. You will be that much closer when the time comes to book it.

Your US cash will not work for you everywhere in South Africa. When you travel to Africa, you don't want to carry any more cash than you have to. If you want to use a credit card, the PHs will usually charge an additional fee to offset the one being imposed on them by the credit card company, usually 5 to 7 percent. You could take cash or traveler's checks to pay for any extra animals or souvenirs that you may want to bring back. But remember that you may need to exchange them for the South African rand as most places will not accept your American cash for payment, like your PH. You may be able to make the exchange in the US airport before you leave.

I hope that you can now understand that an African safari is a doable hunt for the everyday workingman. Theoretically speaking, you can do your safari for the price of a "trophy" elk or whitetail hunt if you figure in all the little overlooked incidentals. As for myself, as I said before, I hunt on public land for free and save up my money for the African experience. And remember, the deer or elk hunt will only get you one animal. The same money spent on safari will yield half of a dozen!

Most people think that to go on safari, you need to have ten or fifteen thousand dollars in hand before you ever book your hunt. While this is a wonderful thing most people are not able to spend money in this fashion. Your safari can be paid out over a period of time, and I'll show you how. Let's look at the time line for your safari.

OK, let's say you've finally decided to make it happen. After an extensive, lengthy, and educated search, you have settled in on a PH in the year 2012 but you don't plan on hunting until 2014. You will need to put your deposit down (which is usually half of the total safari daily rate) in order to book your hunt and hold your safari dates. Now this gives you about a year and a half to two years to save up for the animals and the rest of the daily rate that you will owe. The balance of the daily rate will be due upon arrival in camp. But you can start wiring the money to the PH before your hunt ever begins. Some PHs may have a US bank account that you simply make a deposit into. A 175 dollars here and three hundred dollars there could have you caught up on the daily rate within the first six to eight months of booking your hunt.

Then work on paying for your animals over the course of the next eighteen months. Very few outfitters are going to say, "Pay me when you get home." You have a price list of all the animals that you want to take so you already know the cost. Also most outfitters will allow you to lock in the current year's prices for your hunt that's scheduled for the next year. Some may be able to hold those prices for you for two years but that's pushing it a little. This way you can kind of beat the inflation curve. The goal that you are going after is to have all your animals paid for before your safari ever begins. If at the end of the safari if you haven't shot all the animals you have paid for, the outfitter will transfer back to you the balance. Most likely he will try to get you to shoot something else toward the last day or so. On the other hand, you may owe him additional money so keep up with your balance. Instead of socks and ties for Christmas for your birthday, ask for safari ammo or money toward a zebra.

Once you've saved and sent enough money for your animals it's time to focus on the taxidermy and the shipping. You will need at least the deposit (which is usually half of the total taxidermy cost) before any work will commence. If you are having your mounts done in South Africa you will have around eight months to a year to pay off the rest of the balance on the taxidermy and the shipping cost. Upon final payment you trophies will be on their way.

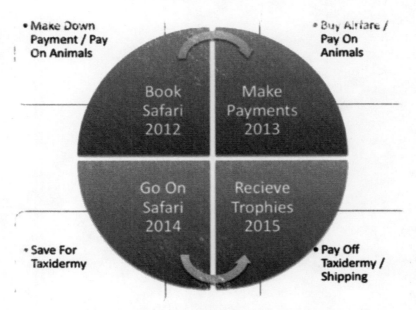

A diagram of the time line for planning your safari.

So you see in this example you first saved up and then booked your hunt in 2012. You worked on paying for your animals in 2013. And then you hunted in 2014. In 2015, you will then finish paying for the taxidermy and shipping. That's a little over four years to pay for the hunt of a lifetime. This is why I say no, this why I know a safari is attainable for the everyday workingman.

Thoughts on the African Safari

For many, the very concept of going on a safari congers up thoughts of a couple of rich gray-haired gentlemen in a remote bush camp surrounded by trackers and gun bearers. They're puffing on big fat cigars, patting each other on the back, and shaking hands while standing over a buffalo or maybe a bull elephant that they just shot. I can assure you that I am not that man. What I am is a man that loves the outdoors and loves to hunt, and even more so, a man that is consumed with a love to hunt Africa.

For years, I have worked and saved, and saved and worked. I have spent what feels like a lifetime waiting for the day that I might make my African dream come true. In the beginning, as a child, it was never my intent to hunt Africa but to only have just one single chance to experience and embrace her beauty. Growing up in the country, I became an avid hunter of small game. My passion quickly grew, as did the size of my prey. Bird hunting turned into rabbits, rabbits into calling predators, and predators into deer. By the grace of God, I managed to get the opportunity to go on my very first safari. The planning was a tremendous undertaking as I wanted every detail to be covered. Traveling for twenty-eight hours and well over eight thousand miles away from home, the plan was to eliminate any surprises. After dreaming of Africa for so many years, I was convinced that there was no way the experience would live up to my expectations. I was pleasantly surprised when the country greatly exceeded all that I had hoped for. After my second safari a few years later, I decided to put something together that would aid others in their planning.

As we all know, the best way to learn about planning a trip like a safari is to talk to someone that has been there and done that. I would like for you to consider this book as your conversation with an old friend. Most of us are not like the hunters on the television hunting shows. In essence, we are not paid personalities; thus, we must pay to play. Our experiences on a safari will be very different from theirs. Our safaris will come to us through great personal sacrifices. In the end, you should reflect back on your time in Africa and say, "Yes, it was a lot of work, but it was worth it, and I can't hardly wait to go back and do all over again!"

I hope the time that we spent here was enlightening and will be of great use to you in the planning of your safari. Thank you for your time and for allowing me to share this information with you.

I'm Kerry Thomas, and on behalf of Paul Stones Safaris in South Africa and myself, shoot straight and good hunting on your hunt of a lifetime!

Safari Planning Checklist

◊ Start saving money.
◊ Decide what you want to hunt.
◊ Decided what part of Africa you want to hunt.
◊ Plan to go to one of the hunter shows.
◊ Gather information on professional hunters and outfitters.
◊ Continue saving money.
◊ Select professional hunter.
◊ Select hunt dates and book it.
◊ Purchase travel insurance.
◊ Make down payment on daily rate.
◊ Get vaccinations if necessary.
◊ Get passport in order.
◊ Book flights and start exercising.
◊ Get quotes on taxidermy, shipping, and importation.
◊ Make payments on daily rate and animals.
◊ Check rates on satellite phone if needed.
◊ Fill out Forms 4457 and SAPS 520.
◊ Get proper gun and ammo cases with TSA locks.
◊ Plan for excursions.
◊ Get packed and make the most of every moment.
◊ Make down payment on taxidermy.
◊ Pay off taxidermy and shipping.

About the Author

Kerry Thomas has spent most of his life in the outdoors enjoying all of what Mother Nature has to offer. He spent two weeks traveling to South Africa in 2008 on his first safari. Like most safari goers, he fell in love with the country. Even before his return, the wheels in his head were already turning working out a plan to return.

During the following three years, he worked out the details with professional hunter Paul Stones for a second safari. On his return trip to hunt with Paul, he took along a videographer and gathered hours upon hours of footage as well as thousands of photographs.

Over the course of the next year, he produced a DVD on how to plan a safari for the budget-minded hunter. His target audience was not the superrich or wealthy but hardworking everyday people like himself. Publishing both a printed book and e-book versions quickly followed up that project.

Currently he continues working as a professional firefighter in the Central Texas area. And to this day, Africa still has a hold on him that is stronger than ever. When he isn't working, he enjoys spending time with his family and teaching his sons about wildlife and nature. In his spare time, he continues to film, photograph, and write about his adventures in the wild.

Made in the USA
San Bernardino, CA
15 December 2013